The
NORMAN ROCKWELL
ILLUSTRATED
COOKBOOK

Created by George Mendoza
Edited by Marian Hoffman

Book Express
Quality and Value in Every Book....

Contents

Soups
and
Chowders

Old-Fashioned Beef-Vegetable Soup

3 pounds shin beef with bone
3 quarts water
2 tablespoons salt
2 teaspoons Worcestershire sauce
¼ teaspoon pepper
1 medium onion, chopped
⅓ cup barley
1 cup celery, chopped
1 cup carrots, sliced
1 cup potatoes, sliced
1 cup cabbage, shredded
1 cup peas
1 turnip, peeled and cubed
3½ cups tomatoes
3 teaspoons parsley flakes

Place beef, water, salt, Worcestershire sauce, and pepper in large pot; cover and simmer 2½ to 3 hours. Remove bone, cut off the meat in small pieces, and return meat to pot.

Add remaining ingredients. Simmer about 45 minutes. *Yield 6 servings.*

Vermont Cheddar Cheese Soup

½ cup carrots, finely diced
½ cup celery, finely diced
½ cup onion, finely diced
½ cup green pepper, finely diced
3 cups Vermont Cheddar cheese, grated
¼ cup butter
¼ cup flour
1 quart chicken broth
2 cups evaporated milk
¼ teaspoon salt
   Pepper to taste
   Sherry or beer (optional)

Sauté vegetables in butter for 5 minutes only, so they remain crunchy. Stir in flour until pasty. Add broth and simmer 5 minutes. Add cheese very slowly; add evaporated milk.

Season to taste with salt and pepper and sherry or beer, if desired. *Yield 6 servings.*

It's good food and not fine words that keeps me alive.

Jean Baptiste Molière 1622–1673

Country-Style Chicken Soup

1   small stewing chicken or 6 backs and
    necks
8   cups water
1   cup celery, chopped
1   cup carrots, sliced
2   medium onions, sliced
1   small bay leaf or ½ teaspoon dill seeds
1   large potato, diced
2   teaspoons salt
¼   teaspoon pepper

Simmer chicken in water 1 to 1½ hours. Add celery, carrots, onions, and bay leaf or dill. Simmer 30 minutes. Remove meat from frame of chicken. Allow meat and vegetables to stand in broth overnight.

Skim off excess fat; add potato and salt and pepper. Simmer 30 minutes longer. You can use leftover chicken to make this soup and omit letting it stand overnight. *Yield 6 servings.*

Chicken Chowder

    Carcass and giblets of 1 chicken
3   pints boiling water
1   onion, peeled and sliced
3   stalks celery with leaves, chopped
1   carrot, peeled and diced
1   teaspoon salt
1   (1-pound) can cream-style corn
1   hard-boiled egg, finely chopped
1   cup flour
¼   teaspoon salt
1   egg

Break up carcass; put with giblets into large kettle. Add boiling water, onion, celery, carrot, and salt; cover. Simmer about 1½ hours.

Remove pieces of carcass and giblets. Cut off all meat; return to pan. Add corn; simmer 10 minutes. Add hard-boiled egg; adjust seasoning.

Sift flour and salt together. Stir in remaining egg, beating with fork until mixture looks like cornmeal. Drop by spoonfuls into hot soup a few minutes before serving. *Yield 5 or 6 servings.*

New England Clam Chowder

1   quart shucked clams with liquor
3   slices salt pork, diced
2   small onions, minced
2   medium potatoes, diced
1   bay leaf
1   cup water
3   cups milk, scalded
1½   cups half-and-half cream
¼   cup butter
     Salt and freshly ground pepper to taste

Drain clams; reserve liquor; chop coarsely.

Fry salt pork slowly in kettle until all fat is rendered. Add onions and sauté until golden. Add potatoes, bay leaf, and water; simmer until potatoes are tender.

Strain reserved clam liquor; stir into potato mixture with milk, cream, butter, and chopped clams. Add seasonings; simmer 15 minutes. Add more seasonings, if needed. Remove bay leaf before serving. *Yield 6 to 8 servings.*

Dilled Crab Chowder

1   large onion, minced
4   stalks celery, minced
8   tablespoons butter
1   pound crabmeat
5   cups milk
1   cup half-and-half or light cream
2   cans cream of potato soup
1   (16½-ounce) can cream-style corn
3   tablespoons pimiento, diced
½   teaspoon salt
1   teaspoon dried dillweed
2   bay leaves
½   cup dry vermouth

In large pot, cook onion and celery in butter until soft. Add crab; stir and add milk, half-and-half, potato soup, corn, pimiento, salt, dill, and bay leaves. Mix well and heat over medium heat for 20 minutes—do not boil. Add vermouth and heat for 5 additional minutes.

Soup can be reheated and stores well in refrigerator 4 to 5 days. *Yield 10 servings.*

Looking Out to Sea - 1927

Hearty Lentil Soup

2   cups lentils
8   cups water
½   cup onion, chopped
2   cloves garlic, minced
½   cup carrots, chopped
½   cup celery, chopped
¼   cup olive oil
1   teaspoon salt
½   teaspoon pepper
3   tablespoons tomato paste
2   bay leaves
½   teaspoon oregano
3   tablespoons wine vinegar
½   cup fried salt pork, diced (optional)

Wash and pick over lentils; soak overnight in 2 cups water.

In Dutch oven or soup kettle, sauté onion, garlic, carrots, and celery in oil. Add lentils, 6 cups water, salt, pepper, tomato paste, bay leaves, and oregano; bring to boil. Cook 2½ to 3 hours, until lentils are soft. Remove bay leaves.

At this point, mixture can be pureed until smooth. Thin with water if necessary. Return mixture to soup pot; heat. Add vinegar. Garnish, if desired, with crisp salt pork cubes. *Yield 8 servings.*

Cape Cod Cranberry and Orange Soup

1   pound fresh cranberries (or canned
     equivalent)
2   cups light chicken stock (or water)
1½   cups white wine
2   or 3 pieces lemon rind
     Pared rind of ripe orange
½   cinnamon stick
¼   to ½ cup sugar to taste
     Juice of 2 oranges
     Juice of ½ lemon
2   envelopes gelatin (if soup is to be jellied)
4   to 6 thin slices orange

Wash cranberries, if fresh; put into pan with stock and wine. Add lemon and orange rind and cinnamon stick; simmer about 10 minutes, until cranberries have softened. Put fruit and juice through fine nylon sieve or fine food mill after removing cinnamon stick; sweeten to taste. Add orange and lemon juice. (If using canned cranberries, it may not be necessary to add any sugar; these are usually sweetened.)

This soup can also be served jellied if 2 envelopes gelatin are softened in little stock or water and added after soup has been sieved. Reheat soup a few minutes while blending in gelatin.

Serve chilled or jellied with orange as garnish. *Yield 4 to 6 servings.*

Cream of Corn Soup

3   tablespoons butter
1   onion, chopped
1   medium potato, finely sliced
1½   cups fresh or canned corn
3½   cups milk
1   bay leaf
3   or 4 sprigs parsley
     Salt and pepper
¼   teaspoon mace
1   chicken bouillon cube
4   to 6 teaspoons heavy cream
1   tablespoon chives or parsley, chopped
     Croutons

Melt butter. Cook onion and potato gently, about 5 minutes; shake pan occasionally to prevent sticking. Add 1 cup corn; stir well. Add milk, bay leaf, parsley, salt, pepper, and mace; bring to simmer. Add bouillon cube; cook until vegetables are tender. Put into electric blender or food processor and blend until smooth.

Return to pan with remaining corn (if fresh, simmer in salted water until tender). Reheat until nearly boiling; adjust seasoning. Serve in soup cups with spoonful of cream, sprinkling of chives, and croutons in each cup. *Yield 4 to 6 servings.*

Mushroom-Shrimp Chowder

1   pound fresh mushrooms, sliced
1½ cups water
2½ teaspoons salt
¼   cup fresh onion, chopped
¼   cup butter, melted
¼   cup all-purpose flour
⅛   teaspoon freshly ground pepper
2½ cups milk
½   cup whipping cream
2   cups cooked shrimp, chopped
     Parsley

Combine mushrooms, water, and 1 teaspoon of the salt in a saucepan and bring to a boil. Reduce heat and cover. Simmer for 10 minutes, then drain mushrooms and reserve liquid.

Sauté onion in butter in a saucepan until tender. Add flour, remaining salt, and pepper and mix well. Stir in reserved liquid gradually, blending until smooth, then add milk gradually and cook, stirring constantly, until mixture comes to a boil and thickens. Remove from heat and stir in cream, shrimp, and mushrooms. Chill thoroughly before serving. Garnish with parsley. *Yield about 6 servings.*

He was a bold man that first eat an oyster.

Jonathan Swift 1667–1745

Man with Harpoon - 1940

Oyster Bisque

1   quart fresh oysters
3   cups Basic Chicken Stock (see Index)
1½ cups fine bread crumbs
⅓   cup onion, finely chopped
1   cup celery, finely diced
     Salt and white pepper to taste
1   quart milk, scalded
2   tablespoons butter
¼   cup sherry

Drain oysters and reserve liquid. Chop oysters. Pour chicken stock in soup kettle. Add reserved oyster liquid, bread crumbs, onion, celery, salt, and pepper. Boil slowly, stirring frequently, for about 30 minutes.

Process in blender container or food processor until onion and celery are pureed, then return to soup kettle. Add oysters and heat thoroughly, but do not overcook. Stir in milk, butter, and sherry and heat through. Serve immediately. *Yield 6 to 8 servings.*

Hearty New England Oyster Stew

1   pint oysters
4   tablespoons butter
½   teaspoon salt
     Pepper to taste
     Dash of Tabasco sauce
1   pint milk
1   pint light cream
2   teaspoons butter
     Paprika

Drain oysters; reserve liquor.

Melt 4 tablespoons butter in heavy saucepan; add salt, pepper, and Tabasco. Add reserved liquor to pot; stir to blend well. Add oysters; cook only until edges begin to curl, about 3 to 5 minutes. Stir in milk and cream; bring to boil, but do not boil.

Spoon soup into hot bowls; dot each bowl with butter and healthy dash of paprika. *Yield 4 servings.*

Tell me what you eat, and I will tell you what you are.

Anthelme Brillat-Savarin 1755–1826

Lobster Bisque

1   large lobster (or 2 small, preferably female, lobsters), freshly boiled
5   to 6 cups fish stock
1   small onion, sliced
1   carrot, sliced
2   stalks celery, sliced
1   bay leaf, 3 or 4 sprigs parsley, tied together
     Salt and pepper
5   tablespoons butter
2½   tablespoons flour
¼   teaspoon mace or nutmeg
1   cup cream
3   to 4 tablespoons sherry (or brandy)

Split freshly boiled lobster down back with sharp knife; remove intestine, which looks like long black thread down center of back. Remove stomach sac from head and tough gills. Crack claws; remove meat and add to back meat. If lobster is female and there is red coral or roe, reserve for garnish. Reserve greenish curd from head. Break up all lobster shells; put into pan with stock. Add onion, carrot, celery, herbs, salt, and pepper; cover. Simmer 30 to 45 minutes.

Meanwhile, cut lobster meat into chunks. Pound coral roe with 2 tablespoons butter to use as garnish and to color soup.

Melt 3 tablespoons butter in pot; stir in flour until smoothly blended. Cook a minute or two. Add strained lobster stock; blend until smooth. Bring to boil, stirring constantly. Reduce heat and simmer 4 to 5 minutes. Add lobster meat. Remove herbs. Add mace; adjust seasoning. Add cream and sherry.

Serve in soup cups with piece of coral butter in each cup; sprinkle with paprika. *Yield 6 servings.*

Pea Soup with Ham

3   medium onions
3   whole cloves
1   pound yellow peas
4   cups water
1   pound ham
1   teaspoon marjoram
1   teaspoon thyme
     Salt to taste
     Parsley

Dice 2 onions. Peel third onion, but leave it whole. Stick cloves into whole onion. Put diced onions, whole onion, peas, and water into pot; cook 20 minutes. Add ham, marjoram, and thyme; cook at least 1½ hours.

Remove cloved onion and ham. Cut ham into thick slices. Season soup with salt. When ready to serve, place ham slice on top of each serving of soup; garnish with parsley. *Yield 4 to 6 servings.*

Gone Fishing - 1930

Old-Fashioned Green Split Pea Soup

1   (1-pound) package green split peas
1   ham hock
12 green onions or scallions
1   cup carrots, diced
1   cup celery, diced
1   slice of lemon
½   teaspoon white pepper
    Salt to taste
1   bay leaf

Place peas in colander and rinse thoroughly with cold water. Rinse ham hock with cold water. Place peas, ham hock, and 2½ quarts of water in large kettle or saucepan. Slice green onions, using about 6 of the green tops. Add onions, carrots, celery, lemon, seasonings, and bay leaf to peas mixture. Bring to a boil, then reduce heat. Simmer, uncovered, for 2 hours, stirring frequently to prevent sticking and adding more water as needed. Caution must be taken to avoid scorching as soup thickens.

Remove ham hock, lemon slice, and bay leaf when soup is done. Cut ham from ham hock, discarding skin and bone. Dice ham coarsely, and return it to the soup. Soup may be pureed, if creamier soup is desired. *Yield 6 to 8 servings.*

Halloween Pumpkin Soup

2   tablespoons butter
2   tablespoons onion, chopped
½   teaspoon ginger
1   tablespoon flour
2   cups prepared pumpkin
2   cups Basic Chicken Stock (see Index) or 2
    chicken bouillon cubes in 2 cups water
2   cups milk
    Salt to season

Sauté butter, onion, and ginger. Stir in flour. Add pumpkin; cook 5 minutes. Gradually add stock and milk; simmer 5 minutes.

Season with salt. *Yield 4 servings.*

Hearty Seafood Stew

Sauce
2   tablespoons vegetable oil
2   onions, chopped, or 3 leeks, sliced
4   cloves garlic, crushed
2   fresh tomatoes, peeled and diced
3   tablespoons tomato paste
2   cups bottled clam juice
4   cups chicken bouillon
1   tablespoon salt
⅛   teaspoon pepper
¼   teaspoon saffron
½   teaspoon thyme
1   bay leaf
6   sprigs parsley
    Grated rind of 1 orange

Seafoods
1   (2-pound) lobster and/or other shellfish
    (clams, mussels with shells, scallops, crab,
    shrimp)
2   pounds assorted whitefish fillets, such as
    sea bass, perch, cod, sole, flounder, red
    snapper
    Chopped parsley (garnish)

Heat oil in large saucepan or Dutch oven; sauté onions several minutes, until translucent. Add remaining sauce ingredients and simmer 45 minutes.

Prepare seafoods. Cook lobster. (Place in large kettle of boiling salted water 10 minutes.) Break claws and tail from body; crack claws. Cut tail into 1-inch chunks. Remove black vein from tail pieces; leave shell on meat. Wash fish fillets; cut into 2-inch pieces. Add lobster and firm-fleshed fish (sea bass, perch, etc.) to boiling sauce; cook 5 minutes. Add tender-fleshed fish, such as clams, scallops, sole, or cod; cook 5 minutes. Lift seafoods out as soon as cooked; keep warm in soup tureen or platter.

Boil liquid 10 minutes to reduce; strain through coarse sieve into tureen. Mash through some of vegetables. Garnish with parsley. *Yield 6 servings.*

Winter Night Turkey-Vegetable Soup

1 small onion, chopped
2 tablespoons butter or margarine
2 cups water
2 chicken bouillon cubes
2 cups cooked turkey, diced
½ cup celery tops and pieces
1½ cups potatoes, diced
1 cup carrots, diced
2½ cups milk
2 tablespoons flour
1 teaspoon salt
⅛ teaspoon pepper

Cook onion in butter until tender. Add water, bouillon cubes, turkey, and vegetables. Boil gently, covered, until vegetables are tender.

Stir a little milk into flour until mixture is smooth. Add remaining milk, salt, and pepper; add to soup. Simmer, stirring occasionally to prevent sticking, until soup is slightly thickened. *Yield 6 servings.*

Basic Beef Stock

3 pounds beef brisket
2 pounds medium soupbones
5 quarts water
4 green onions and tops
1 large onion, studded with 10 cloves
1 celery stalk and leaves
1 Bouquet Garni (optional) (see Index)
2 tablespoons salt

Place beef and bones in large baking pan. Bake at 400°F for about 1 hour, or until well browned on both sides. Remove from pan and place in large stock pot. Drain off fat from baking pan; add 1 cup water to pan and scrape up brown bits from bottom. Pour into stock pot.

Add remaining water and remaining ingredients, except salt. Bring slowly to a boil, removing scum as it accumulates on surface. Cover and simmer for 1 hour. Add salt. Simmer for 3 hours longer. Remove meat and vegetables. Strain through wet muslin. Chill and remove fat before using. *Yield 2½ quarts.*

Basic Chicken Stock

1 (4-pound) hen
1 pound chicken wings
2 tablespoons salt
4 peppercorns
5 quarts water
½ bay leaf
 Pinch of thyme
6 green onions with tops
4 large carrots, quartered
2 stalks celery with leaves, cut in 2-inch pieces
1 large onion, studded with 3 cloves

Place chicken, salt, peppercorns, and water in stock pot. Bring to boil over medium heat, removing scum from surface. Cover pot and reduce heat. Simmer for 1 hour, skimming frequently. Add remaining ingredients; cover and cook for about 2 hours and 30 minutes. Skim off fat; season to taste with additional salt and pepper.

Remove chicken and vegetables from stock. Strain stock through wet muslin. Chill and remove fat before using. *Yield 2½ quarts.*

Serenely full, the epicure would say,
Fate cannot harm me; I have dined today.

Sydney Smith 1771–1845

Bouquet Garni

1 parsley stalk
1 bay leaf
2 sprigs of thyme
1 sprig of marjoram (optional)

Combine all ingredients in a small piece of muslin or a double thickness of cheesecloth; tie securely with string.

Fish and Seafood

Freshly Caught Fish with Mushroom Stuffing

Mushroom Stuffing
3   tablespoons butter
1   small onion, chopped
½   cup fresh mushrooms, chopped
2   cups dry bread crumbs
¾   cup chicken stock
1   egg, beaten
½   teaspoon salt
¼   teaspoon pepper

1   (4-pound) whole fish of your choice, dressed
1   teaspoon salt
4   strips bacon

Prepare Mushroom Stuffing. Put butter in saucepan. Add onion; sauté until golden but not brown. Add mushrooms; cook until water from mushrooms cooks away. Remove from heat. Add bread crumbs, chicken stock, egg, ½ teaspoon salt, and pepper; mix well with hands.

Clean and rub inside of fish with 1 teaspoon salt. Stuff fish; fasten with toothpicks. Place, underside-down, in greased baking dish; layer bacon over fish. Bake in 350°F oven 1 hour, or until fish flakes easily. Remove to hot platter to serve. *Yield 8 servings.*

Friday Dinner Fish Cakes

1   egg
1   tablespoon lemon juice
1   onion, finely minced
2   tablespoons prepared mustard
½   teaspoon salt
¼   teaspoon pepper
1   teaspoon parsley flakes
1   pound cooked fish, boned and flaked
¼   to ½ cup cornflake crumbs
    Fat for deep frying

Mix egg, lemon juice, onion, and seasonings in bowl; toss with fish. Add enough cornflake crumbs so fish cakes shape easily. Roll each cake in extra crumbs to coat outside.

Heat fat in medium skillet; fry cakes until crisp and brown on outside. Drain on paper towels; place on heated platter. Serve with sautéed chopped celery and scallions. *Yield 4 to 6 servings.*

Fish dinners will make a man spring like a flea.

Thomas Jordan 1612–1685

Contentment - 1926

16

Gussied-Up Codfish Cakes

1   cup cooked codfish, shredded
1   cup mashed potatoes
2   eggs, slightly beaten
½   teaspoon freshly ground pepper
1½   cups fine bread crumbs
¼   cup butter
1   (10½-ounce) can cream of shrimp soup
1   tablespoon soy sauce

Combine codfish, potatoes, eggs, and pepper and blend well. Shape codfish mixture into 8 cakes and coat well with bread crumbs. Melt butter in skillet. Fry cakes in butter until lightly browned on both sides, then arrange on serving platter. Heat soup and soy sauce in saucepan over low heat, stirring frequently. Spoon soup mixture over codfish cakes and garnish with fresh dill sprigs and lemon wedges. *Yield 8 servings.*

Cape Cod Turkey

1   pound salt cod
4   large red or yellow onions, finely sliced
⅔   cup white vinegar
⅔   cup water
2½   tablespoons sugar
     Salt and pepper to taste
4   pounds medium boiling potatoes
¾   pound lean salt pork, finely diced

Cover cod with cold water and let soak overnight. Drain and rinse well. Combine onions, vinegar, water, sugar, salt, and pepper in bowl and let stand for about 2 hours before serving time.

Peel potatoes and cut in half, then place in a 5-quart boiler. Place cod over potatoes and add enough water to cover. Cover with lid and bring to a boil. Reduce heat and simmer for about 40 minutes, or until potatoes are tender.

Place diced pork in iron skillet and cook slowly over medium heat until golden brown. Pour diced pork and fat into gravy boat. This is the sauce.

Drain potatoes and cod and arrange on platter. Spoon pickled onions over potatoes and cod. *Yield 4 to 6 servings.*

New England Baked Cod

1   dressed fresh cod (scrod), about 2 pounds
3   lemons
4   tomatoes, sliced
1   pound whole mushrooms
½   teaspoon salt
⅛   teaspoon pepper
½   teaspoon marjoram
½   teaspoon thyme
1   bay leaf
1   large onion, cut into rings
3   tablespoons vegetable oil

Wash fish; pat dry. Place in baking dish; sprinkle with juice of 1 lemon. Garnish with tomatoes and remaining lemons (sliced).

Wash mushrooms; place around fish. Season with salt and pepper; add marjoram, thyme, and bay leaf. Add onion; sprinkle with oil. Bake, covered (foil or lid), 15 minutes in preheated 325°F oven. Remove cover and cook 10 to 15 minutes, until fish flakes. *Yield 4 servings.*

New Englander's Cod and Oyster Scallop

1   pound cod or fish fillets
1   pint oysters, drained
½   cup butter or margarine
2   tablespoons onion, finely chopped
¼   teaspoon liquid hot pepper sauce
3   cups saltine crackers, crushed
2   tablespoons parsley, chopped
¼   teaspoon salt
⅛   teaspoon pepper
1   cup half-and-half cream

Cut fish into 1-inch cubes.

Melt butter in saucepan. Add onion; cook until tender. Stir in pepper sauce.

Combine onion, crackers and parsley. Place ⅓ of crumb mixture in bottom of well-greased 1½-quart casserole. Place ½ the fish and oysters on crumb mixture. Sprinkle with ½ the salt and pepper. Repeat layers; end with crumb mixture. Pour cream over contents in dish. Bake in 400°F oven 25 to 30 minutes, until fish flakes easily. *Yield 6 servings.*

East Coast Baked Bluefish

2 pounds bluefish fillets
½ cup milk
   Salt and pepper
1 cup dried bread crumbs
¼ pound butter
2 tablespoons lemon juice
   Seafood seasoning to taste (about ½ cup)

Place fillets into large pot cold water with about 3 tablespoons lemon juice. Cover pot; place in refrigerator overnight. This draws oil out of bluefish. Bluefish tend to taste oily, so it is important to do this before baking.

Heat oven to 500°F.

Dip fillets in milk; lightly salt and pepper. Dip into bread crumbs. Place ½ teaspoon butter on each fillet; sprinkle with lemon juice. Sprinkle with seafood seasoning. Place in well-buttered pan. Bake uncovered 10 to 12 minutes, until fish flakes easily. *Yield 6 servings.*

*When I make a feast,
I would my guests should praise it,
not the cooks.*

Sir John Harington 1561–1612

The Catch - 1929

Weekend Angler's Fillet of Flounder

1½ pounds fillets of flounder
    Salt and pepper
¾   cup fine bread crumbs
1   egg
    Butter or oil

Wipe fillets with cold, damp cloth; sprinkle with salt and pepper. Dip in crumbs, then in slightly beaten egg, diluted with water, and again in crumbs. Cook in small amount butter in frying pan 8 to 10 minutes, until brown on both sides. Garnish with lemon and parsley; serve with Tartar Sauce (see Index). *Yield 4 servings.*

Boston Baked Haddock

2 pounds haddock fillets
2 teaspoons lemon juice
   Dash of pepper
6 slices bacon, chopped
½ cup soft bread crumbs
2 tablespoons parsley, chopped
¾ cup onion, thinly sliced
2 tablespoons bacon fat

Skin fillets; place in single layer in greased 12 × 8 × 2-inch baking dish. Sprinkle with lemon juice and pepper.

Fry bacon until crisp; remove from fat. Add to bread crumbs and parsley.

Cook onion in bacon fat until tender; spread over fish. Sprinkle crumb mixture over onion. Bake in 350°F oven 25 to 30 minutes until fish flakes easily. *Yield 6 servings.*

Fisherman's Paradise: Haddock with Mussels

2   pounds haddock, cod, or other thick fillets
4   pounds (about 4 dozen) mussels in shells
    (clams can be substituted)
1   cup dry white wine
1   cup water
1   small onion, sliced
½   teaspoon salt
½   cup whipping cream
¼   cup butter or margarine
    Dash of white pepper
    Dash of nutmeg
2   tablespoons parsley, chopped
    Parslied potatoes
1   cup each zucchini, carrots, and celery, cut
    julienne style
    Butter or margarine for cooking vegetables

Cut fillets into serving-size portions.

Clean mussels in cold water. Scrub shells with stiff brush; rinse thoroughly several times.

Combine wine, water, and onion in large pan; bring to simmering stage. Add mussels. Cover; steam about 5 minutes until shells open. Remove mussels from shells; set aside.

Strain cooking liquid into large skillet; add fillets and salt. Cover; simmer 8 to 10 minutes, until fish flakes easily. Transfer fillets to warm platter; keep warm.

Reduce cooking liquid to ½ cup. Stir in whipping cream, ¼ cup butter, pepper, and nutmeg; simmer until sauce thickens slightly. Add mussels and parsley; heat. Spoon mixture over fillets. Serve with parslied potatoes and julienne strips of zucchini, carrot, and celery sautéed in butter; stir constantly just until tender. *Yield 6 servings.*

I never lost a little fish—
yes, I am free to say
It always was the biggest fish
I caught that got away.

Eugene Field 1850–1895

Busy-Day Halibut

2   pounds (¾-inch thick) halibut or other
    firm steaks or fillets
2   tablespoons dry onion soup mix
1   cup dairy sour cream
1   cup fine dry bread crumbs
2   tablespoons Parmesan cheese, grated
1   tablespoon parsley, chopped
¼   teaspoon paprika
¼   cup melted butter, margarine, or oil

Thaw fish if frozen; dry well. Cut into 6 portions. Combine soup mix and sour cream. In separate bowl mix bread crumbs, cheese, parsley, and paprika.

Dip fish in sour-cream mixture; roll in bread-crumb mixture. Place in single layer on well-greased shallow baking pan. Pour butter or oil over fish. Bake in 500°F oven 10 to 12 minutes, until fish flakes easily. *Yield 6 servings.*

Note: Seasoned Italian bread crumbs can be used in place of bread crumb-cheese mixture.

Fried Smelts

2   pounds smelts, heads off, cleaned, and
    washed
2   eggs, beaten
2   tablespoons milk
1   teaspoon salt
¼   teaspoon pepper
½   cup flour
½   cup dried bread or cracker crumbs
    Tartar Sauce (see Index)

Drain smelts as dry as possible on paper towels. Mix eggs, milk, and seasonings in bowl. Mix flour and crumbs together on large piece of waxed paper. Dip each smelt in liquid, then in crumb mixture.

Deep fry at 370°F 3 to 5 minutes; turn each fish once. Do not fry too many at a time. Drain on paper towels; season.

If using skillet, sauté in butter or oil (or both), allowing 1½ to 2 minutes on each side. Drain; season. Serve with Tartar Sauce. *Yield 4 to 6 servings.*

Boned Mackerel with Lemon Sauce

5   small mackerel, cleaned
1   cup fine soft bread crumbs
2   tablespoons chopped chives
2   tablespoons parsley, freshly minced
1   slice bacon, finely chopped
     Grated rind and juice of 1 lemon
     Salt and freshly ground pepper to taste

Have fish dealer remove heads and tails from mackerel; bone without cutting mackerel in half. If this is not possible, cut off head and tail; slit fish down underside. Remove entrails; rinse fish. Lay mackerel open; lift out bones in one piece, using a small, sharp knife.

Combine bread crumbs, chives, parsley, bacon, lemon rind and juice, salt, and pepper in bowl; mix well. Divide into 5 equal parts; shape each part into roll that will fit in mackerel cavity. Place 1 roll inside each mackerel; place each mackerel on sheet of lightly oiled aluminum foil. Wrap loosely; seal edges. Place foil packets on baking sheet. Bake in preheated 375°F oven 20 to 25 minutes, depending on size, until mackerel is tender and flakes easily.

Unwrap; arrange on serving platter. Garnish with lemon slices and parsley sprigs. Pour half the Lemon Sauce over mackerel; serve rest hot in sauceboat. *Yield 5 servings.*

Lemon Sauce

½   teaspoon freshly ground pepper
2   cloves garlic, pressed
1   tablespoon dried tarragon
1   teaspoon salt
2   tablespoons parsley, freshly minced
2   lemons, cut into sections
1   cup vegetable oil
1   tablespoon wine vinegar

Place pepper, garlic, tarragon, salt, and parsley in blender container; blend. Add oil very slowly, alternating with drops of vinegar; blend well after each addition. Place in top of double boiler.

Cut lemon sections into small pieces; add with any juice to sauce. Mix well; place over hot water until heated through. *Yield about 1¼ cups.*

Barbecued Oysters

3   dozen large oysters in shells
     Bread crumbs
     Paprika
½   pound bacon, thinly sliced

Wash oyster shells thoroughly. Open oysters; discard flatter shell. Separate oysters from curved shell, but allow each to remain loosely in shell. Cover oysters with bread crumbs; season with paprika. Cover each with bacon.

Place (in their shells) in one layer under broiler flame until bacon is cooked through. Serve in shells. *Yield 6 servings.*

Broiled Oysters

24   oysters
     Melted butter
     Dried bread crumbs
6   slices toast, cut into uniform pieces
     Salt and pepper
     Few drops of lemon juice

Dry oysters between towels. Heat broiler; grease pan well. Dip oysters in butter, then in crumbs; arrange on broiler. Broil about 3 minutes.

Moisten toast with hot oyster juice; place 4 broiled oysters on each slice. Season with salt, pepper, and lemon juice. *Yield 6 servings.*

Down Home Fried Oysters

1   pint oysters
     Salt
     Pepper
     Flour for dredging
1   egg, slightly beaten
½   cup cracker or bread crumbs

Pick over oysters, removing shell fragments; dry between towels. Sprinkle with salt, pepper, and flour. Dip in egg diluted with a little cold water. Roll in crumbs.

Fry in deep, hot (375°F) fat 4 to 6 minutes. Drain on unglazed paper. *Yield 4 servings.*

Fisherman's Baked Red Snapper

1   (5-pound) red snapper, cleaned and boned
1   teaspoon salt
1   pound boiled shrimp
1   egg
1   cup cream
½   tablespoon anchovy paste
    Pepper
    Paprika
1   cup sherry

Wash and drain fish; rub with salt. Put shrimp through grinder or chop in food processor. Beat egg and half the cream together.

Mix shrimp and anchovy paste; season with pepper, salt, and paprika. Stir into egg and cream. Add sherry; mix to smooth paste.

Place stuffing inside fish; sew together with twine or fasten with kitchen skewers. Place in baking dish; pour over remaining ½ cup cream. Bake in 350°F oven until done, about 4 hours. Serve garnished with sliced cucumbers in French dressing. *Yield 10 servings.*

The Worm - 1961

Summer Evening Grilled Red Snapper Steaks

2   pounds red snapper steaks
½   cup melted fat or oil
¼   cup lemon juice
2   teaspoons salt
½   teaspoon Worcestershire sauce
¼   teaspoon white pepper
     Dash of liquid hot pepper sauce
     Paprika

Pat fish dry with paper towels. Cut into serving-size portions; place in well-greased, hinged wire grills.

Combine remaining ingredients, except paprika. Baste fish with sauce; sprinkle with paprika. Cook about 4 inches from moderately hot charcoal coals or broiler 8 minutes. Baste with sauce; sprinkle with paprika. Turn; cook 7 to 10 minutes, until fish flakes easily. *Yield 6 servings.*

Stuffed Fillet of Sole

2   pounds boiled spinach or 1 package frozen
     spinach
1   teaspoon salt
⅛   teaspoon pepper
½   cup dry white wine
¼   cup bread crumbs
6   fillets of sole
½   cup onion, finely chopped
2   tablespoons parsley, finely chopped
2   tablespoons butter
1   cup mushrooms, sliced
2   medium tomatoes, peeled and quartered
2   tablespoons flour
¼   cup whipped cream
1   tablespoon lemon juice

Drain spinach; chop. Add salt, pepper, ⅓ cup wine, and bread crumbs. Place mound on one end of each fillet; fold other end over it. Place in well-greased baking pan with onion, parsley, and remaining wine. Arrange mushrooms and tomatoes over top; cover with cooking parchment paper. Bake in 500°F oven 15 minutes. Remove fillets to heatproof platter.

Thicken gravy remaining in pan with flour blended with a little cold water. Simmer 2 or 3 minutes, stirring constantly. Remove from heat; add whipped cream and lemon juice. Pour over fillets; brown in broiler. Serve immediately. *Yield 6 servings.*

Trout Dinner

6   dressed fresh trout
2   bay leaves, halved
1   small shallot, thinly sliced
4   peppercorns
2   or 3 sprigs of parsley
     Salt
½   cup wine vinegar
½   cup water
1½   cups soft bread crumbs
1   egg, beaten
2   tablespoons parsley, freshly minced
1   tablespoon chopped chives
     Pepper to taste
     Melted butter
1   tablespoon capers
1   small lemon, cut into sections

Have fish dealer remove heads and tails from trout, then bone without cutting in half. Place trout in shallow glass container. Combine bay leaves, shallot, peppercorns, parsley, and 1 teaspoon of salt and sprinkle over trout. Mix vinegar and water and pour over trout. Marinate in refrigerator overnight. Drain trout and reserve marinade.

Combine crumbs, egg, 1 tablespoon of parsley, chives, salt to taste, and pepper in a bowl and mix well. Stuff trout cavities with the dressing, then brush trout with melted butter. Arrange trout in shallow baking dish and cover lightly with aluminum foil. Bake in preheated 375°F oven for about 20 minutes, or until trout flakes easily when pierced with fork.

Strain reserved marinade and place in small saucepan. Stir in capers, remaining parsley, lemon sections, and marinade mixture. Heat through. Arrange trout on a serving dish and pour the sauce over the trout. Serve hot. *Yield 6 servings.*

Sport - 1939

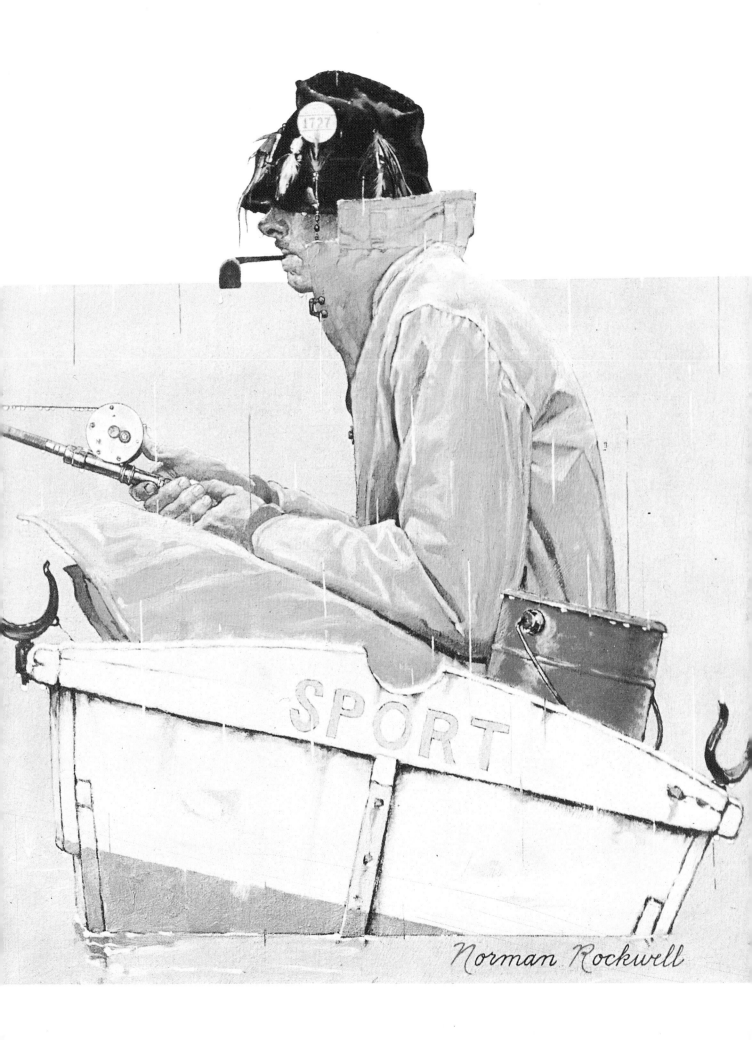

Pilgrims' Clam Pie

3   dozen shell clams
1½   cups water
¼   cup margarine or butter
½   cup fresh mushrooms, sliced
2   tablespoons onion, minced
¼   cup all-purpose flour
¼   teaspoon dry mustard
⅛   teaspoon liquid hot pepper sauce
¼   teaspoon salt
⅛   teaspoon white pepper
1   cup reserved clam liquid
1   cup half-and-half cream
1   tablespoon lemon juice
2   tablespoons parsley, chopped
2   tablespoons pimiento, chopped
     Pastry for 1-crust, 9-inch pie
1   egg, beaten

Wash clam shells thoroughly. Place clams in large pot with water; bring to boil. Simmer 8 to 10 minutes, until clams open. Remove clams from shells; cut into fourths. Reserve 1 cup clam liquid.

Melt margarine in skillet. Add mushrooms and onion; cook until tender. Stir in flour, mustard, pepper sauce, salt, and pepper. Gradually add clam liquid and cream; cook, stirring constantly, until thick. Stir in lemon juice, parsley, pimiento, and clams; pour into 9-inch-round deep-dish pie plate (about 2 inches deep).

Roll out pastry dough; place on mixture in pie plate. Secure dough to rim of pie plate by crimping; vent pastry. Brush with beaten egg. Bake in 375°F oven 25 to 30 minutes, until pastry is browned. *Yield 6 servings.*

Maryland Crab Imperial

1   green sweet pepper, minced
1   medium onion, minced
2   teaspoons dry mustard
2   teaspoons prepared horseradish
2   teaspoons salt
½   teaspoon freshly ground white pepper
2   eggs, beaten
1   cup Basic Mayonnaise (see Index)
3   pounds lump crab meat
     Paprika

Combine green pepper, onion, mustard, horseradish, salt, white pepper, and eggs and mix well. Blend in mayonnaise thoroughly, then fold in crab meat. Spoon crab meat mixture into 8 large cleaned crab shells or ramekins. Coat with additional mayonnaise and sprinkle generously with paprika.

Arrange crab shells in shallow oblong baking pan. Bake in preheated 350°F oven for 15 to 20 minutes, or until heated through. *Yield 8 servings.*

Baked Scallops

1   pound scallops
2   tablespoons shallots or green onions, chopped
6   tablespoons butter
1   teaspoon lemon juice
⅓   cup fine bread crumbs
2   tablespoons parsley, chopped

Wash scallops to remove sand; dry on paper towels. Place in 4 buttered shells or buttered casserole.

Sauté shallots in 2 tablespoons butter until soft; distribute evenly over scallops.

Melt remaining butter; add lemon juice. Pour over scallops; sprinkle with crumbs. Bake in preheated 375°F oven 12 to 15 minutes, until scallops are tender when pierced with knife. Serve very hot; garnish with parsley. *Yield 4 servings.*

Broiled Scallops

2½   pounds scallops
     Corn oil
½   cup butter, melted
     Juice of 1 large lemon
3   to 4 tablespoons green onions (scallions), finely chopped

Prepare scallops; marinate about 1 hour in enough oil to coat all sides. Drain; put into preheated shallow pan. Sprinkle with salt and pepper.

Mix butter with lemon juice and onions; baste scallops continuously while cooking, about 5 to 6 minutes. *Yield 6 servings.*

Point Judith Scallops

1   pound scallops
½   cup butter or margarine
1   cup fresh mushrooms, sliced
2   tablespoons onion, minced
2   tablespoons all-purpose flour
½   teaspoon salt
1½   cups half-and-half cream
4   egg yolks, beaten
½   teaspoon leaf thyme
¼   teaspoon basil leaves
½   cup fresh bread crumbs
⅓   cup Swiss Gruyére cheese, grated
¼   teaspoon paprika
1   tablespoon butter or margarine, melted

Remove shell particles from scallops; wash. Melt ¼ cup butter in skillet. Add scallops and mushrooms; cook 3 to 4 minutes, until scallops are done. Divide scallops and mushrooms among 6 individual shells or ramekins.

Melt ¼ cup butter in small saucepan. Add onion; cook until tender. Stir in flour and salt. Gradually stir in half-and-half; cook until thickened, stirring constantly. Add a little hot sauce to egg yolks; add to remaining sauce, stirring constantly. Heat just until thickened. Stir in thyme and basil. Spoon sauce over scallops.

Combine crumbs, cheese, paprika, and 1 tablespoon butter; sprinkle on sauce. Place shells on baking tray. Bake in 400°F oven 10 to 15 minutes, until hot and bubbly. *Yield 6 servings.*

Baked Mussels

   Mussels
   Salt
   Pepper
   Onion, chopped
   Bacon strips
   Grated cheese

Scrub mussels; open shells with knife, like clams. Remove beard; lay in baking pan. Sprinkle with salt, pepper, and onion. Lay bacon on top. Sprinkle with cheese.

Bake in 300°F oven until bacon is crisp. *Yield about 8 mussels per serving.*

Boiled Maine Lobster

1½   gallons water
⅓   cup salt
6   live lobsters (1 pound each)
   Melted butter or margarine

Pour water into large kettle. Add salt; cover. Bring to boiling point over hot coals or high heat. Plunge lobsters headfirst into boiling water; cover. After water has returned to boiling point, simmer 15 to 20 minutes, depending on size of lobsters. Test lobsters by taking hold of a leg; if it detaches easily, lobster is cooked. Do not overcook.

Drain; crack claws. Serve with melted butter. *Yield 6 servings.*

And do as adversaries do in law, Strive mightily, but eat and drink as friends.

William Shakespeare 1564–1616

Special Night Lobster Newburg

6   tablespoons butter
2   tablespoons flour
3   cups cooked lobster, cut up
1   teaspoon nutmeg
   Dash of paprika
1   teaspoon salt
3   tablespoons sherry
3   egg yolks
2   cups cream
   Toast triangles

Melt butter over low heat in top of double boiler; stir in flour, lobster, nutmeg, paprika, salt, and sherry.

Beat yolks lightly in small bowl. Add cream; mix well. Slowly stir yolk mixture into lobster. Cook over hot water, stirring, until just thickened. Serve on toast or serve in individual shells topped with buttered fresh bread crumbs and browned under broiler. *Yield 6 servings.*

Baked Stuffed Shrimp

1   pound extra jumbo or lobster shrimp
¼   cup milk
1   egg
½   cup bread crumbs
½   teaspoon paprika
1   pound lump crab meat
1   teaspoon Worcestershire sauce
    Salt and pepper to taste
1   teaspoon Tabasco sauce
1   teaspoon mustard
1   tablespoon mayonnaise
2   slices white bread, cubed into small pieces
1   medium onion
½   green pepper, finely chopped
½   cup butter or margarine, melted

Shell uncooked shrimp; leave tail shell on. Split shrimp down back; spread apart, butterfly fashion. Dip uncooked shrimp into milk and egg mixture. Next dip in bread crumbs and paprika mixture.

Combine crab meat, Worcestershire sauce, salt, pepper, Tabasco sauce, mustard, mayonnaise, and bread cubes. Sauté onion and green pepper in 2 tablespoons melted butter; add to crab meat mixture.

Firmly stuff breaded shrimp with crab meat mixture. Place shrimp, tail-side-up, on greased, shallow baking dish. Baste with butter. Bake in 400°F oven 30 to 40 minutes, until brown. *Yield 5 servings.*

French-Fried Butterfly Shrimp

2   pounds large raw shrimp
1   cup all-purpose flour, sifted
½   teaspoon sugar
    Dash of curry powder
1   egg
1   cup water
2   teaspoons salad oil
½   teaspoon salt

Peel shrimp; leave tail on. Slit shrimp along back; remove sand vein. Flatten; make cut in back. Pull tail through; pat dry.

Combine dry ingredients; add egg, water, and oil; beat well. Dip shrimp in batter; fry in hot fat until golden brown. Remove to paper towels. Serve immediately. *Yield 4 to 6 servings.*

Note: For an appetizer, serve with chutney and lemon wedges. For main course, serve with chili or tartar sauce.

We may live without poetry, music and art;
We may live without conscience, and live without heart;
We may live without friends; we may live without books;
But civilized man cannot live without cooks.

Owen Meredith (E.R.B. Lytton, Earl of Lytton)

1831–1891

Beef

Sunday Dinner Beef Roast

3   pounds beef brisket
4   slices bacon, diced
1   cup onions, chopped
8   cups stale bread cubes
1   teaspoon oregano
¼   cup parsley, finely chopped
2   eggs, lightly beaten
    Salt and freshly ground pepper to taste

Have the butcher cut a large pocket in brisket. Sauté bacon for about 3 minutes; then add onions and cook, stirring frequently, until lightly browned. Combine bread cubes with bacon mixture in large mixing bowl and toss lightly. Add oregano, parsley, and eggs and toss with fork until well combined. Season with salt and pepper, then sprinkle about 3 table-spoons of water over the stuffing if mixture seems too dry. Pack stuffing evenly into pocket of the brisket. Secure opening with skewers. Score top of roast lightly, sprinkle pepper over roast and rub it in. Place in lightly greased, shallow baking pan. Cover loosely with aluminum foil. Bake in preheated 350°F oven for 1 hour and 45 minutes. Remove foil and bake for 30 minutes longer.

Remove from oven and place on serving platter; pour pan juices over top of roast, if desired. You may double the recipe for the stuffing and bake additional amount separately, if desired. *Yield 8 to 10 servings.*

Old Country Beef with Sauerkraut

2½ to 3 pounds beef brisket
3   tablespoons bacon fat
1   large onion, peeled and sliced
2   pounds sauerkraut
2   cups boiling water
    Salt and pepper
    Few caraway seeds

Heat fat in pan. Add onion; sauté until lightly browned. Put in meat; arrange sauerkraut on top. Add boiling water; cover. Simmer over low heat 2 to 2½ hours, or until meat is tender.

Add salt and pepper to taste and a few caraway seeds. Serve with boiled potatoes. *Yield 6 servings.*

Summer Days - 1952

30

Boiled Beef and Carrots

3   to 4 pounds bottom round of beef
1   large onion stuck with 2 cloves
6   peppercorns
1   bay leaf
     Parsley stems
     Sprig of thyme
     Salt
8   to 10 medium carrots
2   small turnips
3   celery stalks
4   to 6 small onions, whole

Dumplings
2   cups flour (all-purpose)
8   tablespoons suet (or butter)
3   tablespoons parsley, chopped
½   tablespoon thyme
½   tablespoon marjoram
     Pepper

Put beef, large onion, peppercorns, bay leaf, parsley stems, sprig of thyme, enough water to cover meat, and a little salt into a large pot. Slowly bring to boil, removing any scum that rises to surface. Put lid on pot; simmer 1 hour.

Peel and quarter carrots and turnips lengthwise. Remove herbs and large onion from pot. Add carrots, turnips, celery, and small onions to pot; simmer 1 hour.

Make dumplings: Sift flour with pinch of salt. Mix in finely shredded suet, herbs, and pepper. Mix in water to make light dough. Divide into pieces about size of small walnut, rolling between hands. Drop dumplings into boiling liquid around meat; cover pot. Cook about 15 to 20 minutes.

Serve on large dish with vegetables and dumplings. Serve gravy separately in sauceboat. *Yield 6 servings.*

And the people sat down to eat and to drink, and rose up to play.

The Bible

New England Boiled Dinner

3   to 4 pounds corned-beef brisket
1   clove garlic, minced
1   bay leaf
6   medium potatoes
3   carrots, cut in halves
2   small onions, cut in quarters
1   small head cabbage, cut in sixths

Place corned beef in Dutch oven; barely cover beef with water. Add garlic and bay leaf; bring to boil. Reduce heat; simmer, covered, until meat is tender when pricked with fork, about 3 to 4 hours.

Remove meat from broth; keep warm. Add potatoes, carrots, and onions to broth. Cover; cook 10 minutes. Add cabbage; cook, covered, 20 minutes. Remove bay leaf. *Yield 6 servings.*

Fancy Grilled Hamburgers

1   tablespoon butter
1½   teaspoons olive oil
1   medium onion, minced
1   pound extra lean ground beef
3   drops of hot sauce
1   tablespoon Worcestershire sauce
1   teaspoon salt
½   teaspoon freshly ground pepper
2   egg yolks, lightly beaten
⅔   cup soft bread crumbs
      Basic Barbecue Sauce (see Index)

Melt butter with olive oil in small frying pan. Add onion and sauté until golden. Combine ground beef, onion, hot sauce, Worcestershire sauce, salt, and pepper in a bowl and mix well. Add egg yolks and bread crumbs, mixing until well combined. Shape meat into 4 patties, 3 inches in diameter and about ½ inch thick.

Place patties on grill rack about 4 inches above the hot charcoal (or under a preheated broiler). Sear meat quickly on both sides. Raise grill rack to 6 to 8 inches above the coals and cook for 5 minutes on each side. Serve with Basic Barbecue Sauce. *Yield 2 servings.*

Batter-Dipped Beef Hot Dogs

½ cup cornmeal
½ cup flour, sifted
1 teaspoon salt
½ teaspoon pepper
½ cup fluid milk
1 egg, beaten
2 tablespoons melted fat or oil
12 all-beef hot dogs
  Fat or oil for deep frying

Mix cornmeal, flour, salt, and pepper in bowl. Add milk, egg, and fat; stir until smooth. Dip hot dogs into batter; drain over bowl.

Fry in heated fat for 2 to 3 minutes, until golden brown, turning once. Remove from fat; drain. *Yield 6 servings.*

"Company's Coming" Broiled Sirloin

4 (1-inch-thick) sirloin steaks
½ clove garlic
1 teaspoon salt
½ teaspoon freshly ground black pepper
½ cup butter
2 cups mushrooms, sliced

Rub steaks with garlic. Sprinkle with half the salt and pepper. Score fatty edges of steak. Place on broiling pan 3 inches from heat. Broil on one side to desired degree of doneness. Turn; season uncooked side with remaining salt and pepper. Return meat to broiler; cook to desired doneness.

While steak is broiling, melt butter. Add mushrooms; sauté until golden brown and tender.

Arrange steaks on serving platter; cover with sautéed mushrooms. *Yield 4 servings.*

Marinated Beef Roast

1 clove garlic, minced
1 teaspoon freshly ground black pepper
1 bay leaf
1½ cups dry red wine
2 tablespoons lemon juice
1 (4-pound) rolled rump roast
3 tablespoons olive oil
2 tablespoons flour
2 tablespoons water

Combine garlic, pepper, bay leaf, wine, and lemon juice in enamelware pan or deep glass casserole. Add roast; turn several times to coat with mixture. Cover; let marinate in refrigerator at least 24 hours, turning occasionally.

Heat oil over moderate heat. Remove roast from marinade; pat dry. Brown on all sides in hot oil.

Meanwhile, preheat oven to 375°F. Pour marinade over roast in Dutch oven; cover tightly. Place in oven and cook 2 hours. Uncover; bake 30 minutes. Transfer pan to stove; remove meat to warm platter.

Make a paste with flour and water; thicken pan gravy. Slice roast. Serve with gravy and oven-fried potato wedges or boiled or mashed potatoes. *Yield 8 to 10 servings.*

Family Meat Loaf

1½ pounds ground beef
3 slices soft white bread, torn into very small pieces
1 cup tomato juice or milk
½ cup onion, finely chopped
2 tablespoons parsley, chopped
1 egg, beaten
1 teaspoon salt
¼ teaspoon pepper

Mix ingredients thoroughly. Press into 9 × 5 × 3-inch loaf pan or shape into loaf.

Bake uncovered at 350°F about 1½ hours. Remove from oven; drain off excess fat. *Yield 6 servings.*

Norman Rockwell

Hearty Onion and Beef Stew

1¼ pounds stew beef, cut into 1-inch pieces
¼   cup olive oil
2   cups sliced onions or 2 cups small pearl
    onions, peeled
2   cloves garlic, minced
½   teaspoon salt
½   teaspoon pepper
½   teaspoon allspice
½   teaspoon sugar
1   (2-inch) piece cinnamon stick
1⅓ cups dry red wine
1   (8-ounce) can tomato sauce

Brown meat in hot oil in heavy skillet; remove from pan.

Brown onions and garlic. Add other ingredients; stir well. Add meat; bring to boil. Reduce heat to simmer; cover. Cook, stirring occasionally, 2 hours or until meat is very tender. *Yield 4 servings.*

Massachusetts Cranberry Pot Roast

3   to 4 pounds beef arm pot roast, cut 2
    inches thick
2   tablespoons cooking fat, if needed
2   teaspoons salt
¼   teaspoon pepper
4   whole cloves
1   stick cinnamon
½   cup water
3   tablespoons prepared horseradish
6   medium carrots, cut into 2-inch pieces
6   small onions, cut in half lengthwise
½   cup cranberry sauce (whole-berry)
2   tablespoons flour

Brown meat in own fat (trimmed from meat) or cooking fat, in large frying pan. Pour off drippings. Sprinkle salt and pepper over meat. Add cloves and cinnamon. Combine water and horseradish; add to meat. Cover tightly; cook slowly 2½ hours. Turn meat.

Add vegetables to meat. Cook, covered, 40 minutes or until meat and vegetables are tender. Remove meat and vegetables to warm platter.

Blend cranberry sauce with flour; combine with cooking liquid. Cook, stirring constantly, until thickened. Reduce heat; cook 3 minutes. *Yield 6 to 8 servings.*

Note: For beef blade roast, reduce initial cooking time 30 to 45 minutes.

I am a great eater of beef, and I believe that does harm to my wit.

William Shakespeare 1564–1616

Lamb

North Country Lamb Chops

4   large loin or 8 rib lamb chops
1   teaspoon thyme
1   teaspoon oregano
1   teaspoon rosemary
3   small bay leaves, crushed
6   coriander seeds, crushed
     Grated rind and juice of 1 lemon
     Pinch of paprika
6   tablespoons oil
     Salt and pepper
     Butter

Trim chops of excess fat. Mix herbs, lemon rind, and paprika. Rub mixture well into both sides of chops. Arrange chops in large shallow dish; pour lemon juice and oil over them. Season lightly with salt and pepper; set aside in cool place about 3 hours, turning occasionally.

When ready to cook, drain chops well; put on grill over hot coals. Turn once or twice while cooking; allow about 16 to 20 minutes.

If any dried herbs are left over, a good pinch sprinkled over hot coals just before removal of chops will give delicious aroma and improve flavor.

Serve chops with pat of butter on each and a plain tossed salad. *Yield 4 servings.*

Durham Lamb Cutlets

½   pound or 2 cups cold cooked lamb
1   small onion
1   tablespoon butter
½   pound mashed potatoes
1   tablespoon parsley, chopped
1   teaspoon tomato puree
     Salt and pepper to taste
2   tablespoons flour
1   egg
3   to 4 tablespoons dried white bread crumbs
     Fat for deep frying

Grind or chop meat very fine.

Chop onions finely; cook in melted butter until golden brown. Add mashed potatoes and meat to onion. Add parsley, tomato puree, salt, and pepper; cook a few seconds. Turn mixture onto plate to cool. Divide into 8 equal-sized portions; form into cutlet shapes. Roll each in flour; dip into beaten egg until coated all over. Roll in bread crumbs.

Heat fat in deep skillet. When smoking slightly, put 3 or 4 cutlets into frying basket; lower into hot fat. Cook until cutlets are rich brown; drain on paper towel. Keep warm while frying remaining cutlets. Arrange in overlapping circle around hot dish; serve with vegetables and brown or tomato sauce. *Yield 4 servings.*

Yankee Stuffed Lamb Chops

6   double-rib lamb chops
1   (3-ounce) can mushroom slices, drained
2   tablespoons mushroom liquid
1   teaspoon salt
¼   cup dry sherry wine
1   egg, beaten
½   cup bread crumbs
¼   teaspoon white pepper

Using sharp knife, make slit from bone side between rib bones into center of meat on each chop.

Drain mushrooms; reserve 2 tablespoons liquid. Mix together reserved mushroom liquid, ½ teaspoon salt, sherry, egg, mushrooms, and bread crumbs. Stuff chops with mixture. Sprinkle with ½ teaspoon salt and pepper. Broil chops 4 to 5 inches from flame, 12 minutes on each side. Serve immediately. *Yield 6 servings.*

This dish of meat is too good for any but anglers, or very honest men.

Izaak Walton 1593–1683

Apricot-Mint Lamb

1   (6-pound) leg of lamb
2   teaspoons salt
¼   teaspoon freshly ground black pepper
1   large onion or 1 teaspoon onion powder
¼   teaspoon garlic powder
1   bouillon cube, dissolved in 1 cup water
1   cup boiling water (approximately)
½   cup apricot preserves
½   teaspoon mint flavoring
¼   teaspoon summer savory
½   cup dry sherry
1   teaspoon arrowroot

Rub leg of lamb well with salt; brown on all sides in roasting pan over moderately high heat. Drain most of fat from pan. Blend pepper, onion, garlic, and bouillon into remaining pan drippings; stir together well.

Mix boiling water, preserves, mint flavoring, and summer savory. Stir into bouillon mixture; add sherry. Roast in 350°F oven 20 to 30 minutes per pound; baste as needed. Blend arrowroot into pan liquid 30 minutes before removing from pan. Cook and stir often until sauce thickens. *Yield 8 to 10 servings.*

Holiday Barbecued Stuffed Leg of Lamb

1   onion, chopped
½   cup dried apricots, soaked and chopped
3   tablespoons raisins, chopped
3   tablespoons dates, chopped
2   tablespoons nuts, chopped
5   tablespoons cooked rice
2   tablespoons parsley, chopped
1   teaspoon chopped marjoram
     Little lemon rind and juice
     Salt and pepper
1   leg of lamb, weighing 3 pounds after removal of bone
     Little strong stock
1   clove garlic, slivered
     Oil
     Barbecue spice or barbecue sauce

Mix onion with apricots, raisins, and dates. Add nuts, rice, parsley, marjoram, lemon rind and juice, salt, pepper, and enough stock to moisten. Fill stuffing into lamb cavity left by removal of bones; sew up slits.

Insert garlic into small shallow slits cut into surface of lamb with point of sharp knife. Put lamb onto rod of spit; spoon oil over surface. Season well with salt, pepper, and barbecue spice or barbecue sauce. Cook about 1½ hours, until meat is tender and browned; baste with oil and seasoning when necessary. *Yield 4 to 6 servings.*

Norman Rockwell

Grilled Lamb

1   (5-pound) leg of lamb
     Vegetable oil
     Salt
½   teaspoon freshly ground pepper
½   cup water
½   cup red wine
2   tablespoons wine vinegar
1   tablespoon Worcestershire sauce
¼   cup lemon juice
1   teaspoon dry mustard
     Dash of hot sauce
¼   teaspoon paprika
1   clove garlic, pressed
1   medium onion, grated

Rub lamb with 1 tablespoon oil, 1 tablespoon salt, and pepper. Place on grill over low coals or in 325°F oven; cook about ¾ to 1 hour. Turn occasionally; brush with oil.

Combine water, wine, vinegar, Worcestershire sauce, lemon juice, mustard, hot sauce, paprika, garlic, onion, 1 tablespoon oil, and ½ teaspoon salt in saucepan; bring to boil. Brush lamb with sauce; cook about 1 hour, to desired degree of doneness. Turn occasionally; brush with sauce. If using oven, turn on broiler after final brushing to glaze slightly. *Yield about 10 servings.*

Baked Ribs of Lamb

1   (2½-pound) strip of lamb ribs
     Salt and freshly ground pepper to taste
2   tablespoons vegetable oil
1   tablespoon soy sauce
1   tablespoon tomato puree
1   clove garlic, pressed
     Salt and pepper

Have thick, bony side of lamb strip cut through in several places when purchasing ribs.

Sprinkle ribs with salt and pepper; place on rack in roasting pan, meat-side-down. Bake in preheated 350°F oven 30 minutes. Turn; bake 30 minutes.

Combine oil, soy sauce, tomato puree, garlic, salt, and pepper in small bowl; brush over ribs. Bake 30 minutes. Cut ribs into serving pieces. *Yield about 4 servings.*

Peninsula Lamb Shanks

6   (1-pound) lamb shanks
1½   teaspoons salt
¼   teaspoon pepper
3   tablespoons oil
3   tablespoons flour
1   (14-ounce) can chicken broth
1   medium onion, sliced
1   clove garlic, finely minced
4   cups celery, sliced
3   medium tomatoes, cut into wedges
1   tablespoon parsley, chopped

Sprinkle lamb with salt and pepper. Heat oil in Dutch oven. Add lamb; brown well on all sides. Remove lamb; set aside.

Stir flour into oil; brown slightly. Gradually blend in broth and 1¾ cups water; bring to boil. Return lamb to Dutch oven; add onion and garlic. Reduce heat; cover. Simmer 1¼ to 1½ hours, until lamb is tender; remove lamb to warm serving platter.

Add celery to liquid in Dutch oven; cook 10 minutes. Add tomatoes and parsley; cook 5 minutes. Spoon over lamb. *Yield 6 servings.*

The Cruise - 1923

Pork

Farmer's Stuffed Pork Chops

Barbecue Sauce
1½ tablespoons oil
1   onion, chopped
1   clove garlic, crushed
1   teaspoon flour
1   small can tomatoes
1   cup brown stock
2   tablespoons vinegar
2   tablespoons Worcestershire sauce
1   tablespoon tomato chutney
1   tablespoon sugar
1   teaspoon lemon juice
1   tablespoon chopped parsley and thyme
¼   teaspoon celery salt

Stuffing
1   onion, chopped
1   stalk celery, chopped
3   tablespoons butter
2   cups fresh bread crumbs
1   apple, chopped
4   tablespoons chopped parsley, thyme, and a little sage
    Grated rind of ½ lemon
1   small egg, beaten
    Few drops lemon juice

4   good-size pork chops
2   to 3 tablespoons oil

Make Barbecue Sauce. Heat oil; cook onion and garlic, covered, 3 to 4 minutes to soften. Remove lid; brown slightly. Add flour; brown slightly. Add tomatoes and stock; bring to boil. Add all other ingredients and cook 15 minutes. Strain; set aside.

Make Stuffing. Cook onion and celery in butter. Add to bread crumbs together with apple, herbs, and lemon rind. Bind mixture with egg and dash of lemon juice; if too dry, add a little milk or stock.

Make cut in center of side of each chop; be careful to make pocket without piercing top or bottom surface of meat. Push stuffing into pocket. Sew up or skewer slits in chops; pat dry. Brown both sides in a little hot oil; remove. Put into ovenproof dish. Spoon over a little Barbecue Sauce thinned with a little extra stock.

Cook in preheated 350°F oven about 1 hour. Take out; remove threads or skewers. Serve with Barbecue Sauce. *Yield 4 servings.*

Butter and honey shall he eat.

The Bible

Party Pork Chops

8   thick-sliced (¾-inch) pork chops
8   onion slices, about ¼ inch thick
8   fresh lemon slices, about ¼ inch thick,
    from midsections of 2 unpeeled lemons
⅔   cup brown sugar
1¼ teaspoons salt
¼   teaspoon pepper
3   tablespoons fresh lemon juice
⅔   cup chili sauce

Place pork in single layer in baking pan. Place 1 onion slice topped with 1 lemon slice on center of each chop.

Blend remaining ingredients; spoon over each chop. Cover pan tightly. Bake in 350°F oven 1½ hours, or until pork is tender. *Yield 8 servings.*

Pork Fillets

2   pounds pork tenderloin
1   large apple
2   tablespoons almonds, chopped
1   teaspoon sugar
¼   teaspoon cinnamon
¼   teaspoon garlic powder
1   teaspoon salt
¼   teaspoon freshly ground pepper
¼   cup olive oil
½   cup dry red wine
1   cup stock

Slice tenderloin into 6 pieces.

Peel, core, and finely chop apple. Combine apple, almonds, sugar, and cinnamon; mix well.

Make horizontal slash in center of each tenderloin without cutting through. Stuff with apple filling. Press meat together; secure with metal clamps or skewers if necessary. Combine garlic powder, salt, and pepper. Rub tenderloins with mixture.

Heat oil in deep skillet; brown tenderloins on all sides. Add wine and stock; bring to boil. Reduce heat; simmer 1 hour, turning meat at 15-minute intervals. *Yield 4 servings.*

New England Pork Roast with Cranberry Stuffing

1   (6- to 7-pound) pork loin roast
    Salt and pepper
    Poultry seasoning
1   cup boiling water
1   beef bouillon cube
½   cup butter
1   (8-ounce) package herb-seasoned bread
    stuffing
1   cup cranberries, knife-chopped
1   small red apple (unpeeled), cored and
    diced (¾ cup)
¼   cup celery, finely chopped
¼   cup parsley, minced
1   large egg

Have butcher saw off backbone (chine) of roast. Place meat, rib-end-up, on cutting board. Holding meaty side of roast with one hand, starting 1 inch from one end of roast and ending 1 inch from other end, cut slit between meat and rib bones almost to bottom of roast. With fingers pull meaty part slightly away from ribs to form pocket. Sprinkle inside of pocket and outside of roast with salt, pepper, and poultry seasoning.

Into large skillet or medium saucepan, off heat, pour boiling water. Add bouillon cube; stir to dissolve. Add butter and, over very low heat, stir until melted. Remove from heat. Add bread stuffing, cranberries, apple, celery, and parsley; mix well.

Beat egg until thick and pale-colored; mix with stuffing. Spoon stuffing into pocket in roast; put any leftover stuffing into small baking dish. Roast pork on rack in shallow roasting pan in 350°F oven 35 minutes per pound. About half an hour before roast is ready, put baking dish of extra stuffing in oven to heat.

After roast has been removed to hot serving platter, pour off fat in roasting pan. Spoon some drippings over top of stuffing in roast and some over small baking dish of extra stuffing. *Yield 6 servings.*

Pork with Cider

1½ pounds lean boneless pork, cut into 1-inch
    cubes
⅓ cup flour
⅓ cup vegetable oil
1½ cups apple cider or apple juice
2 carrots, sliced
1 small onion, sliced
½ teaspoon rosemary
1 bay leaf
1 teaspoon salt
½ teaspoon pepper

Thoroughly dredge pork with flour. Heat oil in
large frying pan until hot. Carefully add pork;
cook until browned on all sides. Remove pork;
drain on paper towels. Place in casserole.

Drain oil from pan. Pour in cider; heat and stir
to remove browned pieces from pan. Add carrots, onion, rosemary, bay leaf, salt, pepper, and
hot cider to casserole; cover. Bake in 325°F
oven 2 hours, until meat is tender. Remove bay
leaf. *Yield 4 servings.*

Frankfurters with Sauerkraut

1 (1-pound) can or bulk sauerkraut
1 small onion, minced
2 tablespoons bacon drippings
1½ teaspoons caraway seed (optional)
    Freshly ground pepper to taste
1 medium potato, grated
1 pound frankfurters

Place sauerkraut in colander, then rinse thoroughly with cold water and drain well. Sauté
onion in bacon drippings in large frying pan
until transparent but not browned. Add sauerkraut, caraway seed, pepper, potato, and 1
cup water. Simmer, covered, for 30 minutes, or
until liquid is absorbed.

Place frankfurters in steamer pan over hot
water and steam for 20 minutes. Turn sauerkraut into serving dish and arrange frankfurters on top. *Yield 4 to 6 servings.*

The appetite grows by eating.

François Rabelais 1495–1553

Home for Tea - 1958

Country Sausage-and-Apple Casserole

8 cups (about 15 slices) white bread, cubed
1 pound country sausage
1 large onion, diced
1 green pepper, diced
½ cup water
2 large apples, pared, cored, and chopped
1 teaspoon salt

Use stale white bread for cubes, or dry them by
putting in 250°F oven 10 minutes.

Brown sausage in large skillet. Cook until no
trace of pink is in meat. Add onion and pepper;
cook 2 minutes. Stir in bread cubes, water, apples, and salt. Mix together until all is evenly
moist. Turn mixture into well-greased casserole. Cook in 350°F oven 30 minutes, or until
top crusts. *Yield 4 to 6 servings.*

Barbecued Pork Ribs

1½ cups catsup
1½ cups water
¾   cup chili sauce
½   cup vinegar
6   tablespoons Worcestershire sauce
6   tablespoons light brown sugar, firmly
    packed
3   tablespoons fresh lemon juice
1   tablespoon paprika
3¼ teaspoons salt
1   clove garlic, crushed
¼   teaspoon hot-pepper sauce
5   pounds pork back ribs
½   teaspoon pepper
    Thin slices of onion and lemon (optional)

Combine catsup, 1½ cups water, chili sauce, vinegar, Worcestershire sauce, brown sugar, lemon juice, paprika, 2¼ teaspoons salt, garlic, and hot-pepper sauce in large saucepan. Heat to boiling; reduce heat. Simmer 30 to 45 minutes, until sauce is good basting consistency.

Cut meat into 3 to 4 rib portions. Sprinkle with 1 teaspoon salt and pepper. Put on rack in shallow baking pan. Bake at 450°F 30 minutes. Remove from rack; drain off excess fat.

Put ribs in baking pan meaty-side-down; brush with sauce. Reduce oven temperature to 300°F; bake 30 minutes. Turn ribs meaty-side-up; brush with sauce. Top each rib with an onion slice. Bake about 1 hour, brushing frequently with some remaining sauce, until ribs are tender and nicely browned. Add lemon slices to ribs during last half hour of baking. Serve remaining sauce on side. *Yield 6 servings.*

Saturday Night Baked Ham

1   (6-pound) butt end ham
1   tablespoon dark molasses
1   tablespoon brown sugar
15 whole cloves
6   cups all-purpose flour
2¼ cups water
1   recipe Basic Brown Sauce (see Index)

Remove most of the rind from ham. Rub ham with molasses and sprinkle with brown sugar. Stud ham fat with cloves.

Place flour in large mixing bowl and add water gradually, mixing with wooden spoon or your hands until stiff dough is formed. Roll dough out on lightly floured surface into a ¾-inch thick square large enough to completely cover ham.

Place ham, fat-side-up, in center of square and moisten edges of dough. Bring edges of dough up to cover ham, pressing moistened edges firmly and trimming off any excess dough.

Place ham on rimmed baking sheet. Bake in preheated 350°F oven for about 3 hours. Cool ham until able to handle, then break off flour casing with a hammer. Place ham on a platter, then cut into thick slices. Spoon brown sauce over ham slices before serving. *Yield about 12 servings.*

Grilled Ham with Raisin and Cranberry Sauce

1½ to 2 pounds (1-inch-thick) ham slices
    Few cloves
½   cup brown sugar
2   tablespoons cornstarch
1½ cups cranberry juice
½   cup orange juice
½   cup seeded or seedless raisins

Score fat edges of ham at intervals of about 2 inches; insert 2 or 3 cloves in fat.

Mix sugar and cornstarch smoothly with cranberry juice; put into pan. Add orange juice and raisins; bring to boil. Stir constantly until mixture thickens.

Put ham on grid over hot coals away from hottest part; cook about 15 minutes. Turn; brush liberally with glaze. Cook 10 minutes. Turn; brush other side. (Can be put on broiler rack in open pan 3 inches below unit. Allow 10 to 12 minutes on each side; brush with glaze as above.) Brush again just before serving; serve any remaining glaze with ham. *Yield 4 or 5 servings.*

Veal

Veal Breast with Herb Stuffing

Herb Stuffing
3   strips bacon, diced
1   medium onion, diced
1   (4-ounce) can mushroom pieces
¼   cup fresh parsley, chopped
1   tablespoon fresh dill, chopped
1   teaspoon dried tarragon leaves
1   teaspoon dried basil leaves
½   pound lean ground beef
½   cup dried bread crumbs
3   eggs, beaten
⅓   cup sour cream
½   teaspoon salt
¼   teaspoon pepper

Veal
3   to 4 pounds boned veal breast or leg
½   teaspoon salt
¼   teaspoon pepper
1   tablespoon vegetable oil
2   cups hot beef broth
2   tablespoons cornstarch
½   cup sour cream

Prepare stuffing. Cook bacon in frying pan until partially cooked. Add onion; cook 5 minutes.

Drain and chop mushrooms; add to pan. Cook 5 minutes; remove from heat. Let cool, then transfer to mixing bowl. Add herbs, beef, crumbs, eggs, and sour cream; mix thoroughly. Season with salt and pepper.

With sharp knife, cut pocket in veal; fill with stuffing. Close opening with toothpicks. (Tie with string if necessary.) Rub outside with salt and pepper.

Heat oil in Dutch oven or heavy saucepan; place meat in pan. Bake in preheated 350°F oven about 1½ hours, basting occasionally with beef broth. When done, place meat on preheated platter.

Pour rest of beef broth into Dutch oven; scrape brown particles from bottom. Bring to simmer. Thoroughly blend cornstarch with sour cream; add to pan drippings, stirring. Cook and stir until thick and bubbly.

Slice veal breast. Serve sauce separately. *Yield 6 servings.*

Grandpa's Grace - 1938

Veal with Mushrooms

2   pounds boneless veal cutlet or fillet, thinly
     sliced
½   cup flour
1   teaspoon salt
¼   teaspoon pepper
2   tablespoons vegetable oil
3   tablespoons butter
1   pound mushrooms, sliced
6   tablespoons wine
2   tablespoons lemon juice
     Lemon slices for garnish

Gently pound veal into very thin pieces. Mix
flour, salt, and pepper; lightly flour veal. Melt
oil and butter in 10-inch frying pan; sauté veal
until golden brown, about 3 minutes each side.
Remove; keep warm.

Add mushrooms to pan; cook several minutes.
Add wine and lemon juice; boil rapidly to reduce sauce slightly. Pour over veal; garnish
with lemon slices. *Yield 6 servings.*

Veal with Rice and Sour Cream

1½   pounds veal, cut into small pieces
2   tablespoons oil
1   medium onion, chopped
1   clove garlic, minced
1   medium green pepper, chopped
2   tablespoons parsley, minced
1   teaspoon paprika
3   cups beef broth
1   cup uncooked rice
1   cup sour cream
     Salt and pepper to taste

Brown veal in oil. Add onion, garlic, and green
pepper; cook a few minutes. Add parsley, paprika, and broth. Simmer, covered, 15 minutes.
Add rice; stir. Cover; cook 15 minutes. Slowly
stir in sour cream. Season to taste; cover. Cook
15 minutes. Serve hot. *Yield 4 to 6 servings.*

Family Dinner - 1950

Variety Meats

Liver with Bacon

12 slices bacon
2   pounds calves liver, sliced ½-inch-thick
    Salt and pepper to taste

Fry bacon in heavy pan until crisp. Remove to paper towels to drain, then keep warm.

Cook liver in bacon drippings over medium heat until browned on both sides and to desired degree of doneness. Remove to warm platter and sprinkle with salt and pepper. Serve with bacon. *Yield 6 servings.*

Braised Liver and Onions

1½ pounds beef liver, sliced
½   cup flour
2   tablespoons fat or oil
1½ teaspoons salt
¼   teaspoon pepper
1   large onion, sliced
¼   cup water

Remove skin and large veins from liver; coat with flour.

Heat fat in large frying pan over moderate heat; brown liver on one side. Turn liver; sprinkle with seasonings. Cover with onion. Add water; cover pan tightly. Cook over low heat 20 to 30 minutes, or until liver is tender. *Yield 6 servings.*

Braised Oxtails

3   tablespoons butter or fat
1   onion, chopped
2   carrots, sliced
1   small turnip, diced
1   stalk celery, chopped
2   tablespoons flour
2   oxtails
1   teaspoon salt
⅛   teaspoon pepper
2   cloves

Melt butter in saucepan. Add onions, carrots, turnip, and celery. When very lightly browned, stir in flour; blend well.

Cut oxtails into 2- to 3-inch pieces; add to pan. Add salt, pepper, cloves, and 2 cups water. Bring to boil, stirring constantly. Reduce heat; let simmer 2 to 3 hours. *Yield 4 servings.*

Cooked Pickled Tongue

1   (2- to 3-pound) pickled tongue

Wash tongue; cover with boiling water. Cook ½ hour; pour off water. Add fresh boiling water to cover; cook over low heat 2 to 2½ hours, until tender. Test with fork. If water cooks out, add more boiling water during cooking period. Cool, peel. Trim base; slice.

Serve on bed of rice or serve cold with Dijon mustard. *Yield 6 servings.*

Sweet-Sour Tongue

1   fresh (2- to 3-pound) tongue
     Salt to taste
1   onion
1   lemon, thinly sliced
1   cup raisins
¼   teaspoon cinnamon
¼   teaspoon allspice
     Pepper to taste
¾   cup vinegar
1   cup brown sugar
10   gingersnaps

Cover tongue with water; cook with salt and onion until tender. Skin tongue, trim base, and slice.

Strain gravy. Add lemon, raisins, cinnamon, allspice, pepper, vinegar, brown sugar, and gingersnaps (softened in water); boil. Add sliced tongue, and boil a few minutes. *Yield 6 to 8 servings.*

Apricot Tongue

1   small beef tongue
     Water
¼   cup soy sauce
2   cloves garlic, cut

Sauce

⅔   cup brown sugar
¾   cup catsup
¼   teaspoon fresh gingerroot, grated, or ½
     teaspoon powdered ginger
1   tablespoon soy sauce
1   package dried apricots

Place tongue in large pot; add water to cover. Mix in ¼ cup soy sauce and garlic. Bring to boil; simmer 2 to 3 hours until tongue is tender. Cool; remove skin. Trim base. Put back in pot to reheat. Slice before serving.

Make sauce: Combine all ingredients in saucepan; simmer slowly until apricots are soft. Pour sauce over sliced tongue. *Yield 4 servings.*

Breaded Sweetbreads

2   pairs sweetbreads
1   sprig parsley
1   stalk celery
½   teaspoon salt
1   cup fine bread crumbs
1   egg, slightly beaten
2   tablespoons butter and/or oil

Soak sweetbreads in cold water 1 hour; drain. Put in saucepan with parsley, celery, salt, and water to cover; bring to boil. Reduce heat; let simmer 30 minutes. Cool in liquid.

Take out sweetbreads. Remove fat and connective tissue. Cut into small, uniform cutlets. Dip in bread crumbs, then in egg diluted with 2 tablespoons water, and again in crumbs. Fry quickly in butter until brown, turning frequently. Serve with tomato sauce or creamed asparagus tips. *Yield 4 servings.*

He may live without books,—what is knowledge but grieving?
He may live without hope,—what is hope but deceiving?
He may live without love,—what is passion but pining?
But where is the man that can live without dining?

Owen Meredith (E.R.B. Lytton, Earl of Lytton) 1831–1891

Poultry

Deviled Chicken

1   (3-pound) chicken
     Cooking oil or butter
     Sea salt or table salt
     White pepper

Preheat oven to 350°F. Line shallow roasting pan with aluminum foil. Brush chicken with oil; sprinkle lightly inside and out with salt and pepper. Place in prepared pan. Cover loosely with aluminum foil; do not seal. Bake for about 1 hour and 30 minutes, or until tender. Let cool enough to handle easily.

Remove and discard skin. Separate chicken into serving portions and arrange on platter. Chicken may be removed from bones if desired and placed on platter. Cover lightly with aluminum foil and keep warm in 225°F oven. Serve with Devil Sauce. *Yield 4 servings.*

I am a true labourer: I earn that I eat, get that I wear, owe no man hate, envy no man's happiness, glad of other men's good.

William Shakespeare 1564–1616

Devil Sauce

3   to 4 small onions, minced
1   large clove of garlic, crushed
     Bouquet Garni (see Index)
     Basic Chicken Stock (see Index)
⅛   teaspoon white pepper
3   tablespoons butter
3   tablespoons flour
¼   teaspoon curry powder
1   tablespoon water
     Several drops of Worcestershire sauce
1   tablespoon tomato puree

Place onions, garlic, Bouquet Garni, 2 cups stock, and pepper in small saucepan; simmer for 20 minutes. Force onion mixture through sieve into a bowl. Measure, then add enough stock to make 2 cups liquid.

Melt butter in small saucepan; blend in flour. Add stock mixture gradually, stirring until smooth. Combine curry powder and water, stirring, to make a smooth paste. Add curry paste, Worcestershire sauce, and tomato puree to sauce. Cook, stirring frequently, until thick and smooth. Serve over warm chicken.

Yield about 2¼ cups.

Chicken Puffs

6   frozen patty shells
2   (1-pound) chicken breasts
2½   tablespoons butter
2   cups Basic Chicken Stock (see Index)
½   box long-grain and wild rice
2   tablespoons cornstarch
2   tablespoons Sauterne
     Salt and pepper to taste
¼   cup onion, chopped
¼   cup green pepper, chopped
¼   cup slivered almonds
1   (4-ounce) jar sliced mushrooms, drained
1   egg

Thaw patty shells. Brown chicken breasts in 2 tablespoons butter. Add chicken stock and cook over medium heat until chicken is tender. Remove chicken from broth and reserve broth. Remove skin and bones from chicken, then cut chicken into small pieces.

Place remaining butter in a saucepan and add 1¼ cups water. Stir in long-grain and wild rice and bring to a boil. Cover tightly. Cook over low heat for about 25 minutes, or until all water is absorbed; cool.

Pour reserved broth into saucepan and bring to a boil. Mix cornstarch and Sauterne and stir into the broth. Cook until thickened, then season with salt and pepper. Let cool.

Combine chicken, rice, half the broth mixture, onion, green pepper, almonds, and mushrooms and mix well. Roll out each patty shell on floured surface to a 6-inch square. Place ⅙ of chicken mixture in center of each square and fold pastry over, forming triangles. Dampen edges of the pastry and seal with fork. Turn upside down onto cookie sheet. Beat egg with 2 tablespoons water, then brush on the triangles.

Bake in preheated 425°F oven 15 minutes, or until brown. Heat remaining broth mixture and serve with puffs. *Yield 6 servings.*

Broiled Spring Chicken

2   small broilers
     Salt and pepper to taste
½   cup butter, melted
4   tablespoons lemon juice

Remove wing tips from broilers and split from the necks through the breasts, leaving backs together. Place on chopping board and flatten with rolling pin. Season with salt and pepper, then place, skin-side-up, on rack in broiler pan. Combine butter and lemon juice; then brush broilers with the butter mixture.

Place broiler pan 3 or 4 inches from source of heat and broil for 2 minutes. Lower pan to about 10 inches from source of heat and broil for about 40 minutes, or until broilers are tender, turning frequently and basting with butter mixture each time. Place on platter and garnish with endive. *Yield about 2 servings.*

Trying Not to Peek - 1929

Brown Chicken Fricassee

1 (3-pound) chicken, disjointed
   Salt and pepper to taste
½ cup butter
½ to 1 teaspoon thyme leaves
½ to 1 teaspoon leaf marjoram
1 large onion, studded with 12 cloves
½ lemon
¾ cup Burgundy
⅛ teaspoon nutmeg
⅛ teaspoon mace
1 cup half-and-half cream
¼ cup all-purpose flour
3 egg yolks, beaten
¼ cup tomato puree (optional)

Season chicken with salt and pepper and place in large saucepan. Add butter, thyme, marjoram, onion, lemon, Burgundy, nutmeg and mace. Add enough water to cover. Bring to boil, then reduce heat. Cover and simmer for about 30 minutes, or until chicken is very tender. Remove chicken from broth and discard lemon and onion. Cool chicken until easily handled.

Remove skin and bones, then dice chicken coarsely or leave in large pieces. Mix enough cream into flour to make smooth thin paste, and stir into broth. Combine egg yolks with remaining cream and blend into broth gradually, stirring constantly. Cook over medium heat, stirring constantly, until thickened; do not allow to boil.

Stir in the tomato puree and add the chicken. Season with salt and pepper and heat through. Serve with rice or pasta. *Yield 4 servings.*

'Tis not the meat, but 'tis the appetite
Makes eating a delight.

Sir John Suckling 1609–1642

Country Chicken Pie with Biscuit Topping

1 (5-pound) stewing chicken, cut in serving pieces
2 small onions
1 teaspoon salt
¼ teaspoon pepper
   Chicken giblets
4 tablespoons butter
4 tablespoons flour
2 cups chicken stock
¼ cup celery, diced
2 tablespoons parsley, chopped
1 onion, minced

Biscuit Dough
1½ cups flour, sifted with 1½ teaspoons baking powder
   Pinch of salt
1 scant tablespoon butter
¼ cup milk, scant

Place chicken in large pot; add water to cover and onions; cook until chicken is tender, about 2½ hours. Season; remove chicken from broth. Cut meat from bones.

Cook giblets in salted water until tender; drain and mince. Melt butter in skillet, then add flour and a little of the broth. Add celery, parsley, minced onion, giblets, and more chicken stock; cook all together for a few minutes. Season to taste.

Place chicken in buttered baking dish. Pour sauce over all; drop teaspoonfuls of biscuit dough on top (not too close together) to make the crust.

To make biscuit dough, sift flour, baking powder, and salt 3 times. Cut butter into flour, mix, and stir in milk. Roll out lightly on a floured board; cut in shapes.

Bake pie in 450°F oven for 15 minutes, or until biscuit crust has browned. *Yield 8 servings.*

Down Home Fried Chicken with Cream Gravy

Salt, pepper, and garlic salt
1 cup flour
1 (2½- to 3-pound) frying chicken, cut into serving pieces
Fat for deep frying

Cream Gravy
2 tablespoons cornstarch
¾ cup hot chicken broth
½ cup milk, at room temperature
1 teaspoon salt
¼ teaspoon pepper

Mix seasonings with flour; coat each chicken piece. Heat fat in skillet; fry chicken, a few pieces at a time. Cook about 25 minutes per batch of chicken, so that pieces are crisp and crusty. Drain on paper towels; set on warmed platter.

Pour off most fat in skillet; leave about 2 tablespoons.

Mix cornstarch with chicken broth. Add to hot fat, stirring constantly. Gradually add milk, salt, and pepper. When slightly thickened, gravy is ready. Serve with the chicken. *Yield 4 to 6 servings.*

And we meet with champagne and a chicken, at last.

Lady Mary Wortley Montagu 1689–1762

Cornish Hens with Southern Dressing

¼ cup raisins
½ cup Sauterne
1 cup butter
1¼ cups onions, chopped
2 cups Cornmeal Muffins, crumbled (see Index)
1 teaspoon salt
Freshly ground pepper to taste
¼ teaspoon poultry seasoning
2 eggs, beaten
¾ cup pecans, chopped
4 Cornish hens
Melted butter
1 cup wild rice or brown rice
1 pound fresh mushrooms, sliced

Soak raisins in Sauterne overnight. Melt ¼ cup butter in small saucepan. Add ¼ cup onions and sauté, stirring constantly, until tender. Place crumbled muffins in large mixing bowl. Add sautéed onions, raisin mixture, ½ teaspoon salt, pepper, poultry seasoning, eggs, and pecans; mix well.

Brush cavities of Cornish hens with melted butter. Stuff hens with cornbread dressing, then place on rack in shallow, oblong baking pan. Bake in preheated 350°F oven for 1 hour, or until hens are tender, brushing with melted butter every 15 minutes.

Cook wild rice while Cornish hens are baking. Sauté remaining onions in ¼ cup of butter until tender, stirring constantly. Wash rice well, then drain. Pour 3 cups water into top of a double boiler, then add remaining ½ teaspoon salt and bring to a boil. Stir in rice gradually, then stir in onions. Bring to boil again. Place over boiling water, then cover and cook for 30 minutes.

Sauté mushrooms in remaining ½ cup of butter for 5 minutes, stirring frequently. Stir into rice mixture; add more boiling water, if needed. Cover and cook for 15 minutes longer, or until rice is tender and water absorbed. Serve with Cornish hens. *Yield 8 servings.*

Thanksgiving - 1952

Hunter's Wild Duck with Wild Rice

2 wild ducks, dressed
1 recipe Marinade for Game (see Index)
   Salt and freshly ground pepper to taste
¼ cup butter
1 apple, quartered
1 onion, quartered
1 carrot, quartered
3½ cups (about) Basic Chicken Stock (see Index)
1 Bouquet Garni (see Index)
2 green onions, finely chopped
1 cup wild rice
½ cup golden raisins
⅓ cup brandy

Place ducks in shallow oblong dish and pour marinade over ducks. Place in refrigerator and marinate for about 12 hours, turning occasionally. Drain ducks well and pat dry, then sprinkle inside and out with salt and pepper.

Brown ducks on all sides in butter in large skillet. Place half the apple, onion, and carrot in each duck cavity. Place ducks in a casserole to fit snugly and add 1 cup of the chicken stock and the Bouquet Garni. Bake, covered, in preheated 350°F oven for 1 hour and 30 minutes, or until the ducks are tender.

Remove ducks from casserole, then discard apple, onion and carrot. Place ducks on serving platter and keep warm. Skim excess fat from casserole liquid and remove Bouquet Garni. Add enough chicken stock to make 2½ cups of liquid. Pour it into top of double boiler, then add green onions and bring to boil.

Wash rice well and drain. Stir into stock mixture, then add raisins and brandy and bring to a boil again, stirring frequently. Place over boiling water and cover. Cook for about 45 minutes or until rice is tender, stirring occasionally and adding chicken stock, if needed.

Place rice on the platter with ducks. Garnish with watercress and orange slices. *Yield 8 servings.*

Roasted Pheasant with Soubise Sauce

1 dressed pheasant
   Salt and pepper to taste
4 slices bacon
6 small white onions, peeled
10 medium mushroom caps
1 recipe Basic Soubise Sauce (see below)

Sprinkle pheasant generously inside and out with salt and pepper. Wrap bacon slices around pheasant and secure each piece with string. Place on rack in broiling pan. Roast in preheated 350°F oven for 1 hour and 30 minutes, or until pheasant is tender. Baste at 15-minute intervals during last 45 minutes of roasting.

Place onions in steamer and steam for 15 minutes. Add mushrooms and steam for 5 minutes longer.

Place pheasant on a platter, then spoon Soubise Sauce over the top, covering completely. Arrange 4 mushroom caps down center of pheasant. Arrange remaining mushrooms, stem-side-up, around the pheasant and place an onion in each mushroom. Serve any remaining sauce with the pheasant. *Yield 4 to 6 servings.*

Basic Soubise Sauce

4 cups onions, thinly sliced
3 cups milk
¾ cup whipping cream
½ teaspoon salt
⅛ teaspoon white pepper

Place onions in saucepan and cover with milk. Simmer until onions are tender. Strain and return liquid to saucepan. Simmer until reduced to ¾ cup liquid. Stir frequently as liquid reduces and thickens. If liquid should curdle, press through a sieve. Place onions in blender and puree.

Combine reduced liquid, onion purée, and cream in saucepan and heat through, stirring constantly. Season with salt and pepper. *Yield about 2 cups of sauce.*

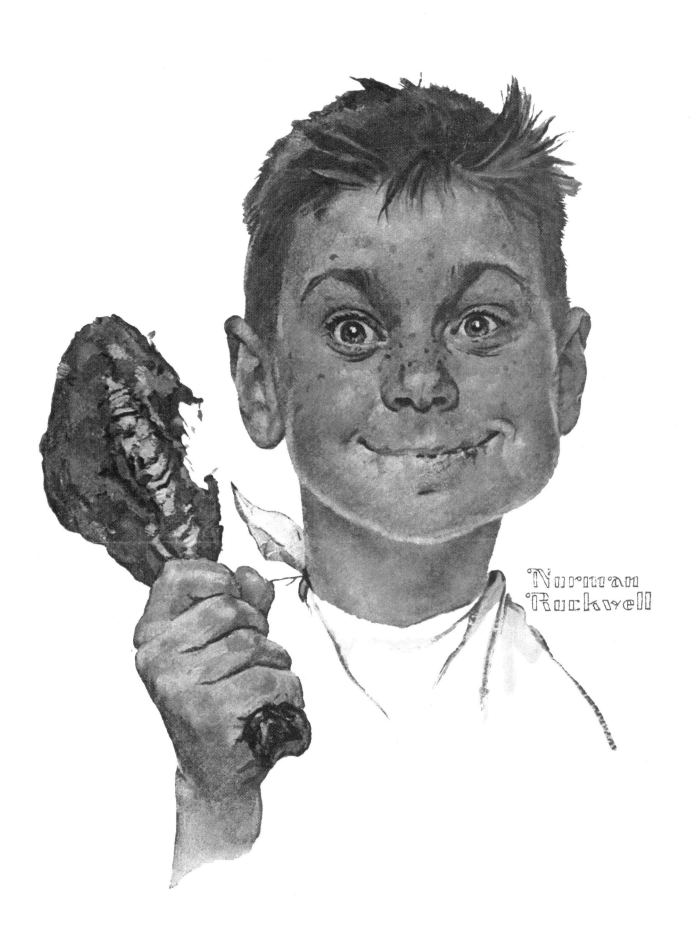

Good Food - 1938

Baked Stuffed Squab

6   dressed squab
1½ teaspoons salt
1   cup celery, chopped
½   cup onion, chopped
3   tablespoons butter
1½ cups boiled rice
6   tablespoons frozen orange juice
       concentrate, thawed
1½ cup fresh mushrooms, chopped
½   cup raisins
1   tablespoon parsley, finely chopped
¾   teaspoon marjoram
¾   cup vegetable oil

Sprinkle squab cavities well with ¾ teaspoon salt. Sauté celery and onion in butter in large skillet until golden; then stir in rice, 3 tablespoons of orange juice concentrate, mushrooms, raisins, parsley, marjoram, and remaining salt. Blend thoroughly and heat through. Spoon rice mixture into squab cavities and truss.

Combine oil and remaining orange juice and blend well. Arrange squab on rack in roasting pan and brush with oil mixture. Bake in preheated 375°F oven for 45 minutes, or until squab is tender, basting frequently with remaining oil mixture.

Arrange squab on serving dish and garnish with parsley and orange slices, if desired. *Yield 6 servings.*

Quail for Six

6   (1-inch) thick slices sandwich bread
       Melted butter
6   slices bacon
6   quail
2   juniper berries, crushed
2   tablespoons sherry
       Salt and freshly ground pepper to taste
1   quart Basic Beef Stock (see Index)
1   tablespoon cornstarch
¼   cup half-and-half cream
       Chopped fresh parsley

Remove crusts from bread slices. Cut 1½-inch angle off each corner of each slice. Hollow out slices by cutting ½ inch from edges of bread halfway to bottom, then remove inside bread to form the cases. Brush all surfaces of each case with butter and place the cases on a cookie sheet. Bake in preheated 450°F oven until well browned, then remove from oven. Reduce oven temperature to 350°F.

Dice bacon and place in a casserole that will hold the quail snugly. Place quail in casserole in single layer and sprinkle crushed juniper berries over quail. Add sherry and season quail with salt and pepper. Cover casserole. Place in oven and bake for 30 minutes, or until quail are tender.

Pour beef stock into 1½-quart saucepan while quail are baking; boil until reduced to 1 cup of stock.

Place bread cases on serving platter, then place quail on bread cases. Keep warm.

Strain casserole liquid into stock in the saucepan and remove excess fat from top. Place saucepan over medium heat. Mix cornstarch with cream until dissolved. Stir into liquid in saucepan and bring to a boil, stirring constantly. Pour over quail and sprinkle with parsley. Garnish with watercress. *Yield 6 servings.*

Best Barbecued Turkey

½ cup onion, chopped
1½ tablespoons butter
1½ cups catsup
¼ cup brown sugar, firmly packed
1 clove garlic, pressed
1 lemon, thinly sliced
¼ cup Worcestershire sauce
2 teaspoons prepared mustard
1 teaspoon salt
¼ teaspoon freshly ground pepper
1 (12-pound) fresh or frozen turkey
2 to 3 tablespoons barbecue salt or seasoned salt

Sauté onion in butter in small saucepan until lightly browned. Add remaining ingredients except turkey and barbecue salt and simmer for 20 minutes. Remove lemon slices. Store sauce in covered jar in refrigerator if not used immediately. Thaw turkey, if frozen. Rinse turkey and pat dry.

Start the charcoal briquette fire 20 to 30 minutes before cooking the turkey, allowing about 5 pounds of charcoal for the beginning fire. During the cooking period, push the burning charcoal to the center while adding more briquettes as needed around the edge.

Sprinkle cavity of turkey with barbecue salt. Truss turkey. Insert spit rod in front of tail and run diagonally through breastbone, then fasten tightly with spit forks at both ends. Test for balance, readjusting spit rod, if necessary. Insert meat thermometer into thickest part of inside thigh, making sure thermometer does not touch the bone or spit rod and that the thermometer will clear the charcoal as the spit turns.

Brush off gray ash from coals and push coals back of the firebox. Place drip pan made of heavy-duty foil directly under turkey in front of the coals. Attach spit and start the rotisserie. Cook for 25 minutes per pound, or to 180 to 185°F on meat thermometer, basting generously and frequently with barbecue sauce during the last 30 minutes of cooking. *Yield 10 to 12 servings.*

Cousin Reginald Catches
the Thanksgiving Turkey

Norman
Rockwell

An Unexpected Turn - 1917

A wonderful bird is the pelican,
His bill will hold more than his belican.
He can take in his beak
Food enough for a week.
But I'm damned if I see how the helican.

Dixon Lanier Merritt 1879–1954

Oven-Smoked Turkey

1   (10- to 12-pound) turkey
¼   cup vegetable oil
½   cup salt
3   tablespoons liquid smoke
1   cup red wine vinegar
¼   cup pepper
2   teaspoons parsley, finely chopped

Rinse turkey, then pat dry with paper towels. Combine oil and salt to make a paste. Rub inside cavity and neck cavity with ¼ cup of the salt paste. Truss turkey, then rub generously with additional oil. Place on one side on a rack in a roaster pan. Bake in preheated 350°F oven for 1 hour.

Combine remaining salt paste with liquid smoke, vinegar, pepper, and parsley. Baste turkey with vinegar mixture, using a basting brush, then turn to other side and baste that side. Bake for 30 minutes, then baste again. Bake for 30 minutes longer, then baste and turn breast-side-up. Baste breast generously. Bake for 2 hours and 30 minutes longer or until tender, basting every 30 minutes.

Let the turkey stand for at least 20 minutes before carving. Brush off some of the salt and pepper before carving. *Yield 10 to 12 servings.*

It is a true saying, that a man must eat a peck of salt with his friend, before he knows him.

Miguel de Cervantes 1547–1616

Roasted Capon

1   (7½- to 8-pound) capon
    Butter
    Salt and freshly ground black peppercorns
    to taste
½   cup water

Rub capon generously with butter, then season inside and out with generous sprinkling of salt and pepper. Truss capon. Place capon in foil-lined baking pan and place on middle shelf of oven at 400°F. Roast for 30 minutes, then spoon up pan juices and baste capon thoroughly. Add water to pan.

Reduce oven temperature to 375°F. Place small piece of foil over breast of capon and bake for about 2 hours longer, basting with pan juices frequently. Test fattest part of thigh by sticking with a slim skewer. If juice is faintly pink, roast for about 15 to 20 minutes longer, or until done. Serve with gravy. *Yield 8 servings.*

Gravy

1½ to 2 cups hot water
3   tablespoons cornstarch

Remove capon to serving dish. Pour pan juices or broth into saucepan and add enough water to broth for desired taste. Combine cornstarch with small amount of broth and mix to a smooth liquid. Pour this into the broth and cook over medium heat, stirring constantly, until slightly thickened and rather clear, or for about 10 to 15 minutes.

Grits, Rice, and Boston Baked Beans

Grits with Cheese

6   cups boiling water
2   teaspoons salt
1½ sticks margarine
1½ cups grits
1   pound sharp Cheddar cheese, cubed or grated
4   eggs, well beaten

Bring water, salt, and margarine to boil; add grits gradually. Cook until thick, stirring constantly. Add cheese; stir until melted. Add eggs; stir rapidly.

Pour into buttered casserole. Bake 1 hour in preheated 250° to 300°F oven. *Yield 8 to 10 servings.*

Note: This can be prepared ahead and baked when needed. Will hold in oven.

Grits Croquettes

2   cups cooked grits
2   cups cooked chicken, meat, or fish, finely chopped
2   tablespoons onion, chopped
1   teaspoon salt
     Pepper to taste
1   teaspoon Worcestershire sauce
     Fine dry bread crumbs
1   egg, beaten
     Fat or oil for deep frying

Combine grits, chicken, onion, salt, pepper, and Worcestershire sauce; chill. Shape into 12 balls or other shape. Roll in bread crumbs; dip in egg. Roll again in bread crumbs.

Heat fat in frying pan. Cook croquettes; turn once to brown each side. *Yield 6 servings.*

Busy-Day Rice Ragout

1   small onion, chopped
1   green pepper, chopped
1   tablespoon oil
1   pound lean ground beef or veal
1   teaspoon salt
     Dash of black pepper
1   tablespoon prepared mustard
2   tablespoons catsup
1   tablespoon Worcestershire sauce
3   cups cooked rice
3   cups canned tomatoes

Use medium to large skillet; stir onion and green pepper in oil until soft. Add meat, salt, and pepper; stir until meat loses pink color. Add remaining ingredients; stir until well blended. Reduce heat; cover skillet. Simmer just 15 minutes. *Yield 4 to 6 servings.*

Orange Rice

3   tablespoons butter
½   cup onion, chopped
1   cup celery, chopped
1   cup long-grain rice
1   cup orange juice
    Grated rind of 1 orange
1½ cups water
½   teaspoon salt
⅛   teaspoon thyme (optional)

Melt butter in medium-size frying pan; then add onions and celery. Sauté until golden but not brown. Combine celery mixture with remaining ingredients in baking dish; cover.

Bake in preheated 350°F oven for 30 minutes, or until liquid is absorbed. *Yield 4 to 6 servings.*

Sugar-and-Spice Rice

1   cup cold water
1   cup whole milk
1   teaspoon salt
1   cup uncooked rice
½   cup butter
½   cup granulated sugar
2   teaspoons cinnamon

Combine water, milk, salt, and uncooked rice in 3-quart saucepan; bring to boil. Stir once; cover. Turn heat very low; cook 20 minutes or until water and milk are absorbed. Do not uncover while cooking.

Spoon rice into serving dishes; top each serving with 2 tablespoons butter, 2 tablespoons sugar, and ½ teaspoon cinnamon. Serve immediately. *Yield 4 servings.*

And they did all eat, and were filled . . .

The Bible, *Matthew*

Boston Baked Beans

1   pound dry navy beans
1   large onion, diced
½   teaspoon salt
1   cup molasses
1   teaspoon dry English mustard
1   teaspoon Worcestershire sauce
1   cup brown sugar, firmly packed
¼   pound salt pork, sliced

Rinse and pick over beans; place in large kettle. Cover with water and let soak 4 hours. Drain; place in large kettle. Cover with water and bring to boil. Cook, covered, about 45 minutes, until just tender. Drain; reserve liquid.

Combine onion, salt, molasses, mustard, Worcestershire sauce, and brown sugar.

Place about ⅓ of beans in bean pot with small amount of reserved liquid. Cover with about ⅓ of molasses mixture. Place several slices pork on top. Repeat layers; add part of reserved liquid with each layer. Bake in preheated 300°F oven 5 to 6 hours, until tender; add water as needed to keep beans covered. *Yield 8 to 10 servings.*

The Hobo - 1924

Egg Dishes

Country Baked Eggs

6   eggs
1¼ cups milk
1   teaspoon salt
2   teaspoons sugar (optional)
1½ tablespoons flour
½   cup cooked ham, finely diced

Beat eggs until light.

Measure milk into 2-cup measure. Add salt, sugar, and flour; mix with eggs. Add ham; pour into buttered baking dish. Bake at 425°F 25 minutes, or until center is firm. *Yield 4 servings.*

Deviled Eggs

6   hard-cooked eggs, peeled
½   teaspoon salt
½   teaspoon dry mustard
¼   teaspoon pepper
3   tablespoons salad dressing, vinegar, or light cream

Cut eggs in half lengthwise. Slip out yolk; mash in small bowl with fork. Mix in seasonings and salad dressing. Fill whites with egg mixture, heaping up highly.

For flavor variation, mix in 2 tablespoons snipped parsley or ½ cup grated cheese. Serve as an appetizer or as a salad. *Yield 6 servings.*

Traditional Scrambled Eggs

2   eggs
2   tablespoons milk or cream
¼   teaspoon salt
     Dash of pepper
½   tablespoon butter

Break eggs into bowl with milk, salt, and pepper. Mix with fork, stirring thoroughly for uniform yellow, or mixing just slightly if streaks of white and yellow are preferred.

Heat butter in skillet over medium heat until just hot enough to sizzle a drop of water. Pour egg mixture into skillet. As mixture begins to set at bottom and side, gently lift cooked portions with spatula so that thin, uncooked portion can flow to bottom. Avoid constant stirring. Cook until eggs are thickened throughout but still moist, about 3 to 5 minutes. *Yield 1 serving.*

Variations: To egg mixture, you can add grated cheese, finely chopped sautéed onions, chopped tomatoes, or chopped green peppers.

A good, honest, wholesome, hungry breakfast.

Izaak Walton 1593–1683

The County Agent - 1948

Farmer's Breakfast

4   **medium potatoes**
4   **strips bacon, cubed**
3   **eggs**
3   **tablespoons milk**
½   **teaspoon salt**
1   **cup cooked ham, cut into small cubes**
2   **medium tomatoes, peeled**
1   **tablespoon chopped chives**

Boil unpeeled potatoes 30 minutes. Rinse under cold water. Peel; set aside to cool. Slice potatoes.

Cook bacon in large frying pan until transparent. Add potatoes; cook until lightly browned.

Meanwhile, blend eggs with milk and salt; stir in cubed ham. Cut tomatoes into thin wedges; add to egg mixture. Pour over potatoes in pan. Cook until eggs are set. Sprinkle with chives; serve at once. *Yield 3 or 4 servings.*

Eggs in Snow

2   **slices bread**
    Butter
    Nutmeg
2   **eggs, separated**
    Salt and pepper
    Grated cheese

Toast bread on 1 side; turn. Toast underside very lightly. Butter lightly toasted side; keep hot.

Add seasoning and pinch of nutmeg to egg whites; beat until stiff. Spread over buttered toast. Make slight indentation in middle; drop in egg yolk. Sprinkle with cheese. Put under hot broiler a few minutes, until egg yolk has set. *Yield 2 servings.*

Retirement Breakfast - 1950

Basic Sauces

Basic Barbecue Sauce

½   cup butter
1   large onion, chopped
½   clove garlic, crushed
1   (14-ounce) bottle catsup
2   tablespoons brown sugar
1   tablespoon Worcestershire sauce
⅓   cup red wine vinegar
1   cup water
¼   teaspoon salt
¼   teaspoon pepper
½   cup cola beverage

Melt butter in saucepan. Add onion and garlic and cook over low heat for about 5 minutes. Add remaining ingredients, except cola beverage, and simmer for about 20 minutes.

Remove from heat and add cola. This sauce is excellent for meats and poultry. *Yield about 3 cups.*

Give me neither poverty nor riches; feed me with food convenient for me.

The Bible, *Proverbs*

Béarnaise Sauce

¼   cup white vinegar
¼   cup dry white wine
1   tablespoon green onion, minced
1   teaspoon dried tarragon
3   peppercorns
3   egg yolks
1   tablespoon warm water
½   cup butter
¼   teaspoon salt

Boil vinegar, wine, onion, tarragon, and peppercorns in small saucepan until liquid has reduced to 2 tablespoons. Pour liquid through fine sieve.

In top of double boiler, over just-simmering water, blend egg yolks and warm water until creamy. (Bottom of double boiler should not touch water.)

Melt butter over low heat. Add by ½ teaspoons to yolk mixture; beat well with wire whip after each addition. (Set bottom of pan in cold-water bath if eggs start to look like scrambled eggs.) After some butter has been added, up to 1 teaspoon butter can be added at one time. Leave white residue in bottom of butter pan. After butter is added, stir in vinegar mixture and salt. *Yield about ¾ cup.*

Basic Brown Sauce

2   tablespoons butter
¼   cup flour
4   cups Basic Beef Stock (see Index)
1   cup tomatoes, chopped
1   cup Mirepoix (see below)

Melt butter in small saucepan; blend in flour to make smooth paste. Cook and stir over low heat, until mixture is browned. Add stock gradually, stirring constantly until smooth. Add tomatoes; simmer for 3 minutes.

Add Mirepoix and simmer until sauce is reduced by half, stirring occasionally. Strain sauce through a fine sieve and serve immediately. *Yield about 3 cups.*

Mirepoix

2   teaspoons butter
2   teaspoons cooking oil
1   medium carrot, coarsely grated
1   medium onion, coarsely grated
1   stalk of celery, finely chopped
⅛   teaspoon dried thyme leaves
1   bay leaf, crushed
2   tablespoons sherry

Melt butter in small heavy saucepan, then add oil. Add carrot, onion, and celery; sauté until soft. Add remaining ingredients; simmer until vegetables are tender. *Yield 1 cup.*

Hollandaise Sauce

½   cup butter
4   egg yolks, well beaten
2   to 2½ tablespoons lemon juice
     Pinch of white pepper
⅛   teaspoon salt

Melt 2 tablespoons butter in top of double boiler; pour gradually into beaten egg yolks, stirring constantly. Return to pan; place pan in or over hot water. Add remaining butter by tablespoons; stir after each tablespoon until melted. Remove from heat; stir in lemon juice, pepper, and salt. *Yield about 1 cup.*

Basic Mayonnaise

4   medium egg yolks
1   teaspoon salt
⅛   teaspoon white pepper
2   cups vegetable oil
1   tablespoon wine vinegar

Place egg yolks, salt, and pepper in medium bowl. Beat with electric hand mixer at medium speed until thick, pale, and fluffy. Add 5 ounces oil in very thin stream, beating constantly, until thickened and oil is absorbed. Beat in vinegar. Add remaining oil slowly, beating constantly, until all oil is blended into mixture. Mayonnaise will be very thick.

Place in refrigerator container. Cut waxed paper to fit over top; rinse in cold water. Place over mayonnaise; cover and refrigerate until ready to use. *Yield 1¾ cups.*

Basic Blender Mayonnaise

1   cup salad oil
1   tablespoon red wine vinegar
1   tablespoon lemon juice
1   egg
½   teaspoon salt
⅛   teaspoon paprika
¼   teaspoon dry mustard
     Dash of cayenne pepper

Pour ¼ cup of oil into electric blender and add vinegar, lemon juice, egg, and seasonings. Cover and blend for 5 seconds. Remove cover while blender is running and add remaining oil in thin steady stream. Turn off blender immediately after adding oil. *Yield 1½ cups.*

Tartar Sauce

1⅔ cups mayonnaise
3   tablespoons sweet pickle, chopped
3   tablespoons stuffed olives, chopped
1   tablespoon capers, chopped
1   tablespoon onion, minced
1   tablespoon parsley, minced
1   teaspoon vinegar
1   teaspoon lemon juice

Combine all ingredients; taste for seasoning. A little extra vinegar or lemon juice and a pinch of salt may be required, depending on kind of mayonnaise used. Serve with any fish or seafood. *Yield about 2 cups.*

Fresh Tomato Sauce

3   medium-size ripe tomatoes, sliced
½   small onion
1   bay leaf
½   cup chicken stock or broth
1   tablespoon butter
1   tablespoon flour
1   teaspoon sugar
¼   teaspoon rosemary, basil, or oregano
½   teaspoon tomato paste (optional)

Simmer tomatoes, onion, bay leaf, and stock 20 minutes. Put into blender 10 seconds; pass through sieve to remove tiny pieces of tomato skins.

Melt butter; add flour. Add 1 cup strained tomato juices gradually; stir with wire whisk until thickened. Add sugar and herbs; simmer 5 minutes. Correct seasoning with salt and pepper. An excellent sauce for spaghetti and other foods. *Yield about 2 cups.*

Note: It may be necessary to add tomato paste in winter months when tomatoes have less flavor.

Basic White Sauce

3   tablespoons butter
3   tablespoons flour
2   cups milk
¾   teaspoon salt
¼   teaspoon white pepper

Melt butter in top of a double boiler over boiling water; stir in flour with wooden spoon until smooth. Add milk gradually, stirring constantly; cook until sauce is thick. Stir in salt and pepper. Remove top of double boiler from water.

Strain sauce through a fine sieve; use as desired. Pour any remaining sauce into small bowl. Cover top of sauce with circle of wet waxed paper; refrigerate for future use. *Yield 2 cups.*

The Night Feeding - 1957

Italian Meat Sauce

¼   cup butter
½   cup olive oil
1½ cups onions, finely chopped
1   cup carrots, grated
½   cup celery, finely chopped
2½ cups mushrooms and stems, finely
    chopped
2   teaspoons parsley, finely chopped
2   pounds lean ground beef
2   tablespoons all-purpose flour
2   tablespoons tomato puree
1   cup red wine
3½ cups beef broth
    Salt and freshly ground pepper to taste

Combine butter and oil in large frying pan; heat. Add onions; sauté 1 minute. Add carrots, celery, mushrooms, and parsley; cook, stirring frequently, 5 minutes. Crumble in ground beef. Cook, stirring frequently, until lightly browned. Sprinkle flour over beef; stir until well blended. Stir in tomato puree.

Add wine gradually, stirring constantly. Add beef broth; season with salt and pepper. Simmer, stirring occasionally, about 1 hour, until thick. Serve with pastas. *Yield about 5 cups.*

Marinade for Beef

1   cup Burgundy
½   cup olive oil
2   parsley stalks
2   sprigs tarragon
2   sprigs thyme
1   bay leaf

Combine all ingredients in small container with lid. Cover and shake to mix well. One-eighth teaspoon dried tarragon leaves and thyme leaves may be substituted for the fresh tarragon and thyme. *Yield about 1½ cups.*

Marinade for Fish

1   cup dry white wine
4   peppercorns
2   teaspoons slivered lemon peel
4   parsley stalks
¼   cup olive oil

Combine all ingredients in small container with lid. Cover and shake to mix well. Marinade may be stored in a covered container in refrigerator. Shake well before using. *Yield about 1¼ cups.*

Marinade for Game

¾   cup port
1¼ cups olive oil
3   sprigs tarragon
2   parsley stalks
1   large celery stalk, coarsely chopped
1   small onion, thinly sliced
6   peppercorns
⅛   teaspoon sage
1   teaspoon lemon peel, slivered

Combine all ingredients in small container with lid. Cover and shake to mix well. Marinate game according to recipe directions. *Yield 2 cups.*

And does not Life consist in sleeping and eating.

Aristophanes 446–380 B.C.

Vegetables

Fresh Asparagus

    20 fresh asparagus
½   cup boiling water
½   teaspoon salt
    Melted butter
    Lemon juice

Cut away fibrous part of asparagus stalks; tie rest together. Place in tall pot; add boiling water and salt. Cover; cook over medium heat about 8 minutes (do not overcook); drain. Add a little lemon juice to melted butter and pour over the asparagus. *Yield 4 servings.*

Harvard Beets

3   tablespoons cornstarch
⅓   cup sugar
¾   teaspoon salt
1½   cups beet liquid (or beet liquid plus water)
2   tablespoons vinegar
1½   tablespoons butter or margarine
3   cups cooked or canned beets, sliced

Mix cornstarch, sugar, and salt; blend in beet liquid, vinegar, and butter. Cook over moderate heat, stirring constantly, until thickened.

Add beets; let stand 10 minutes, if desired, to blend flavors. Heat to serving temperature. *Yield 6 servings.*

Sautéed Broccoli

1   pound fresh young broccoli
    Boiling salted water
3   tablespoons olive oil
1   clove garlic, peeled and chopped
    Salt and pepper to taste

Cut off dry woody stems of broccoli; trim all discolored parts and dead leaves. Separate into small spears; peel stalks with vegetable peeler. Cook 3 to 5 minutes in 1 inch boiling salted water until crisp but tender; drain well.

Heat oil in large skillet over moderate heat. Sauté garlic until lightly browned. Add broccoli; sauté, stirring constantly, 5 minutes. Add salt and pepper. Serve topped with oil from pan. *Yield 4 servings.*

Broccoli Spears with Hollandaise Sauce

1   bunch fresh broccoli
½   teaspoon salt
1   recipe Hollandaise Sauce (see Index)

Cut all but smallest curly leaves away from small heads; cut stems ½-inch long. Cook in small amount of boiling salted water about 12 minutes, until tender; drain well. Place in serving dish; cover with Hollandaise Sauce or serve sauce separately. *Yield 4 servings.*

Grandma's Corn - 1938

Crisp Cabbage

8   cups cabbage, shredded
1   small onion, grated
½   teaspoon sea salt
1   teaspoon dillweed (optional)
¼   cup dill pickle juice (optional)

Combine cabbage, onion, and salt with 1 cup water in Dutch oven or heavy saucepan. Cook, covered, over low heat until cabbage is crisp-tender. Drain, if necessary. Stir in dillweed and pickle juice and serve immediately.

An alternate method is to add butter or cream and pepper to the cooked cabbage, omitting dillweed and pickle juice. *Yield 4 to 6 servings.*

Carrot Loaf

½   cup fine bread crumbs
2½ cups cooked fresh carrots, mashed
2   eggs
1   cup milk
1   teaspoon sugar
½   teaspoon salt
1   teaspoon onion, finely chopped
2   tablespoons butter, melted
¾   cup peanuts, chopped

Combine crumbs and carrots and blend well. Beat eggs and milk together. Add egg mixture and remaining ingredients to carrot mixture. Turn into greased molds or a shallow baking dish, then place in pan of water.

Bake in preheated 350°F oven for 30 minutes. Remove from molds or cut into squares to serve. *Yield 6 to 8 servings.*

Work Can Be Fun - 1921

Young Carrots and Raisins

2   tablespoons butter or margarine
1½   pounds young carrots, scraped and cut
     into ¼-inch slices
⅓   cup water or dry white wine
½   teaspoon ground nutmeg
⅔   cup white raisins
3   teaspoons light brown sugar

Melt butter in medium skillet. Add carrots, water, and nutmeg; cover. Cook over low heat 15 minutes. Stir in raisins and sugar and cook 5 minutes, or until raisins are plump and carrots glazed. *Yield 4 to 6 servings.*

Glazed Carrots

10   to 12 small young carrots, washed and
     trimmed
2   tablespoons margarine
1   tablespoon brown sugar
2   tablespoons honey
2   tablespoons fresh mint

Cook carrots in small amount boiling salted water for 10 minutes. When tender, drain; set aside.

Melt margarine in medium skillet. Add sugar and honey; blend. Add carrots; cook 3 or 4 minutes over low heat, stirring so each carrot is glazed. Sprinkle with mint. Substitute parsley for fresh mint, if preferred. *Yield 4 to 6 servings.*

Brussels Sprouts in Beer

1   pound fresh brussels sprouts, trimmed and
     washed
     Beer (enough to cover sprouts)
½   teaspoon salt
2   tablespoons butter

Place sprouts in medium-size saucepan. Pour over enough beer to cover; bring to boil. Reduce heat; simmer 10 minutes or until tender. Add more beer, if needed, as liquid evaporates; drain. Add salt and butter. Serve hot. *Yield 3 to 4 servings.*

Summertime Fresh Corn on the Cob

6   ears corn, husks and silk removed
     Melted butter
     Salt and pepper to taste

Rinse each ear of corn under cold running water; rub with hands or brush to remove remaining silks. Cut off stems as close as possible to cobs.

Fill kettle ¾ full with water; bring to boil. Add corn, one ear at a time; bring water back to boil. Reduce heat; cover. Simmer 8 to 10 minutes or until corn is tender; drain. Brush with butter; sprinkle with salt and pepper. Force a round, wooden toothpick or corn holder into ends of each ear of corn to serve.

Corn can be placed in baking pan after butter, salt, and pepper have been added, then broiled until lightly browned. Do not place toothpicks or holders in the ends of corn until after broiling. *Yield 6 servings.*

A man hath no better thing under the sun, than to eat, and to drink, and to be merry.

The Bible, Ecclesiastes

Corn Casserole

8   ears of fresh corn, husks and silk removed
2   eggs, well beaten
2   tablespoons onion, grated
¼   cup butter, melted
¾   teaspoon salt
     Dash of pepper
¾   cup milk

Scrape cobs to remove all corn. Add eggs and onion and mix well. Stir in butter, salt, pepper, and milk, then place in buttered baking dish. Bake in preheated 350°F oven for 40 minutes, or until set in center. *Yield 8 servings.*

Fresh Southern Corn Pudding

2   cups fresh corn, cut from cob
2   teaspoons sugar
1½ teaspoons salt
⅛   teaspoon pepper
3   eggs, lightly beaten
2   tablespoons butter
2   cups milk

Combine corn, sugar, salt, and pepper in bowl. Add eggs; mix well.

Place butter and milk in saucepan; heat until butter is melted. Blend with corn mixture. Turn into greased 1-quart casserole; place casserole in pan of hot water. Bake in preheated 350°F oven 1 hour, or until knife inserted in center comes out clean. Garnish with fresh parsley. *Yield 6 servings.*

The Last One - 1938

Cucumbers in Dill

4   cucumbers, peeled and very thinly sliced
1   cup boiling water
¾   cup sour cream
¼   cup lemon juice
3   tablespoons minced dill
1½ teaspoons salt
⅛   teaspoon pepper
1   teaspoon sugar

Pour boiling water over cucumbers; let stand 5 minutes; drain. Plunge into ice water; drain.

Mix remaining ingredients together, pour over cucumbers, tossing until well mixed. Chill 30 minutes before serving. *Yield 6 to 8 servings.*

Garden-Fresh Cucumbers in Sour Cream

4   cucumbers, garden-fresh
1   cup sour cream with chives
1   small bunch leaf lettuce, cleaned
1   tablespoon parsley

Wash cucumbers thoroughly; slice into small wedges. Combine sour cream and cucumbers; mix to coat cucumbers.

Arrange lettuce leaves in salad bowls; pour ½ cup cucumber mixture on lettuce bed. Garnish with parsley. *Yield 4 servings.*

Stuffed Eggplant

2   medium eggplant, cut in half lengthwise
¼   cup salad oil
1   small onion, sliced
¼   cup green pepper strips
1   clove garlic, minced
2   tomatoes, cut in wedges
1   teaspoon oregano
1   teaspoon basil
1   teaspoon salt
     Pepper to taste
¼   cup parsley sprigs

Scoop out pulp from cut eggplant, leaving ½-inch shells. Dice pulp and set aside. Cook eggplant shells in boiling, salted water until just tender; drain. Place in baking dish, cut-side-up. Heat oil in saucepan. Add onion, green pepper, garlic, diced eggplant, tomatoes, oregano, basil, salt, and pepper and cook for about 3 minutes or until heated through, stirring frequently. Spoon into eggplant shells; sprinkle with parsley. Bake at 350°F for 25 minutes. *Yield 4 servings.*

Making Friends - 1935

Fresh Lima Beans in Parsley Cream

3   pounds fresh lima beans, shucked
    Salt and white pepper
2   tablespoons butter or margarine
½   cup cream
1   tablespoon parsley, chopped

Place beans into small saucepan; cover with boiling water. Add 1 teaspoon salt, and cook until tender (20 to 25 minutes unless very small).

Drain well; return to pan. Heat with butter and cream. Season to taste with salt and pepper. Serve in individual bowls; sprinkle with parsley. *Yield 4 servings.*

The First Corn - 1938

Beer-Fried Onion Rings

1½ cups flour
1½ cups beer
4   very large onions, peeled and sliced into
    ¼-inch rounds
    Oil for deep frying

Combine flour and beer in large bowl; blend thoroughly with wooden spoon. Cover bowl; keep at room temperature at least 3 hours.

Divide onion rounds into individual rings. In large skillet, heat enough oil to drop in onion rings. Dip a few onion rings at a time into prepared batter, then into hot (375°F) oil; fry until golden brown. Place on cookie sheet lined with paper towels; keep warm in preheated 200°F oven. Can be frozen and reheated in 400°F oven, if desired. *Yield 4 to 6 servings.*

Eat no onions nor garlic, for we are to utter sweet breath.

William Shakespeare 1564–1616

Northerners' Green Peas

¼   pound Canadian bacon, cut into 1-inch
    pieces
1   tablespoon butter or margarine
3   cups fresh green peas
6   small white onions, peeled
    Inner leaves of lettuce head
½   cup water
½   teaspoon salt
¼   teaspoon pepper
½   teaspoon sugar
1   tablespoon parsley, finely chopped

Fry bacon in butter until lightly browned. Add peas, onions, lettuce, water, salt, pepper, and sugar; cover. Cook 10 to 15 minutes, until peas are tender; drain. Sprinkle with parsley before serving. *Yield 6 servings.*

Green Pepper Salad

2   medium green sweet peppers, seeds and
     membrane removed
3   large firm ripe tomatoes
     Salt and freshly ground pepper to taste
½   cup olive oil
1   to 2 tablespoons red wine vinegar
1½   teaspoons chopped chives
1½   teaspoons parsley, chopped

Cut peppers into thin lengthwise slices. Slice tomatoes thinly.

Arrange tomatoes and peppers in serving dish and sprinkle with salt and pepper. Pour oil evenly over all. Sprinkle vinegar, chives, and parsley over the top. *Yield about 6 servings.*

Community Supper - 1958

Baked Mashed Potatoes

8   medium potatoes, well greased
2   tablespoons butter
½   cup tomato puree
½   cup sour cream
     Salt and pepper to taste
1   cup sharp Cheddar cheese, grated

Bake potatoes in 400°F oven for 45 minutes, or until soft. Split lengthwise, then scoop out centers into mixing bowl. Set shells aside.

Add butter, tomato puree, and sour cream to the potatoes, then mash until well mixed. Season with salt and pepper, then stir in cheese.

Mound potato mixture into the shells and place shells on baking sheet. Broil 10 inches from source of heat until potatoes are heated through. *Yield 8 servings.*

Stuffed Baked Potatoes

4   large baking potatoes, scrubbed and
     greased with oil
2   slices bacon
¼   cup milk
¼   cup butter, melted
     Salt and pepper to taste
2   tablespoons parsley, minced

Bake potatoes at 400°F for 1 hour, or until soft.

Fry bacon until crisp, then drain on absorbent toweling.

Cut potatoes in half lengthwise. Scrape out insides into medium-sized bowl; mash with fork. Stir in milk, melted butter, salt, and pepper. Crumble in the bacon; add parsley and mix well.

Pack mixture into shells and drizzle tops with additional melted butter. Place on cookie sheet. Broil 5 inches from the source of heat until tops are browned. Serve immediately. *Yield 8 servings.*

Hashed Brown Potatoes

3   cups cooked potatoes, cubed
1   teaspoon salt
⅛   teaspoon freshly ground pepper
1   tablespoon onion, minced
¼   cup butter

Sprinkle potatoes with salt, pepper, and onion. Heat butter in skillet. Add potatoes and cook until brown, stirring frequently. Place in serving dish and garnish with parsley. *Yield about 4 servings.*

Homemade Potato Chips

6   medium Idaho potatoes, peeled
      Vegetable oil
      Salt

Cut potatoes very thin on the slicing blade of mandoline or vegetable cutter. Place in large bowl of ice water. Let stand for at least 1 hour. Drain and dry thoroughly on paper towels.

Arrange a layer in frying basket, then lower into hot deep fat. Fry until lightly browned and crisp. Drain, then place on paper towels and sprinkle with salt. *Yield 6 to 8 servings.*

Spicy Sweet-Potato Pie

1½   cups sweet potatoes, cooked and mashed
      into fine paste
½   cup sugar
1   teaspoon cinnamon
1   teaspoon allspice
½   teaspoon salt
3   eggs, well beaten
1   cup milk
2   tablespoons butter, melted
1   9-inch unbaked pie shell

Combine sweet potato paste with sugar, cinnamon, allspice, and salt. Add eggs. Mix milk and butter; stir into potato mixture. Mixture will be fairly liquid. Pour into unbaked pastry shell. Bake at 350°F 40 to 45 minutes. *Yield 6 to 8 servings.*

Sweet-Potato Puffs

2   cups sweet potatoes, mashed
2   egg yolks, beaten
1   cup cream
½   teaspoon salt
2   egg whites, well beaten

Mix potatoes, egg yolks, cream, and salt; heat in saucepan. When very hot, remove from heat. Add egg whites; beat until light. Pile loosely on buttered platter; brush with egg white. Heat in 350°F oven until brown. *Yield 6 servings.*

Fresh Spinach with Bacon

1½   to 2 pounds fresh spinach, washed and
      stems removed
5   slices bacon
½   tablespoon bacon drippings
1   tablespoon lemon juice
½   teaspoon salt
1   hard-boiled egg, chopped

Place spinach in large pan and add ¼ cup water. Cover and cook over medium heat for 10 to 15 minutes, or until spinach is tender, turning occasionally with a fork. Drain well.

Cook bacon until crisp and drain on paper towel. Place spinach in serving dish and crumble bacon over spinach. Add drippings, lemon juice, and salt; toss with 2 forks until mixed. Sprinkle top with chopped eggs. *Yield about 4 servings.*

Baked Spinach with Cheese

1   pound fresh spinach, washed and dried
¼   pound butter
1   large onion, diced
2   cloves garlic, minced
½   teaspoon salt
½   pound Emmentaler cheese, grated
1   teaspoon paprika
⅛   teaspoon nutmeg
¼   teaspoon pepper

Cut spinach into strips. In large Dutch oven or heavy saucepan, heat butter until bubbly. Add onion and garlic; sauté 2 to 3 minutes. Add spinach. Sprinkle with salt; cover. Steam 5 minutes; remove from heat.

Grease ovenproof casserole; sprinkle half the cheese over bottom. Add spinach. Sprinkle with paprika, nutmeg, and pepper. Top with remaining cheese. Bake in preheated 350°F oven about 20 minutes, until cheese bubbles. *Yield 4 servings.*

Stuffed Mushrooms

2   cups fresh spinach
¼   cup Parmesan cheese, freshly grated
2   tablespoons butter, melted
⅛   teaspoon nutmeg
     Salt and pepper to taste
12   large mushroom caps
     Olive oil
12   blanched whole almonds

Cook spinach, then drain thoroughly. Puree half the spinach at a time in a blender. Combine pureed spinach, cheese, butter, nutmeg, salt, and pepper in top of double boiler; mix well. Cover and place over hot, but not boiling, water to keep warm.

Brush entire surface of mushroom caps with oil, then place on baking sheet. Bake in preheated 375°F oven for 10 minutes. Mound spinach mixture inside each mushroom. Garnish with almonds and serve immediately. *Yield 6 servings.*

Marinated Sliced Tomatoes

¼   cup salad oil
1   tablespoon lemon juice
½   teaspoon garlic, minced
½   teaspoon salt
½   teaspoon oregano
4   large tomatoes, peeled and sliced

Combine all but tomatoes; mix well. Pour marinade over tomatoes; marinate several hours. *Yield 3 to 4 servings.*

Broiled Tomatoes

4   medium tomatoes, washed

Garlic Butter
¼   cup butter
1   teaspoon garlic salt
¼   teaspoon white pepper
¼   teaspoon dry mustard

Place tomatoes upside down on broiler pan. With sharp knife, slash skins in "X" design.

Make Garlic Butter. Melt butter; stir in garlic salt, white pepper, and dry mustard. Brush tomatoes with Garlic Butter.

Place broiling pan in farthest slot from flame. Broil tomatoes 2 minutes; remove from broiler. Baste with Garlic Butter. Return to broiler and broil 3 more minutes. *Yield 4 servings.*

Fresh Green Beans with Cherry Tomatoes

1   pound fresh green beans, washed, tips removed, and cut into 1-inch pieces
1¼   teaspoons salt
3   tablespoons butter
½   teaspoon sugar
     Pinch of freshly ground pepper
1½   tablespoons fresh parsley, chopped
8   cherry tomatoes, halved

Place beans in saucepan with 1-inch boiling water and 1 teaspoon salt. Cook 5 minutes; cover. Cook over medium heat 10 to 15 minutes, until just crisp-tender; drain, if necessary.

Add butter, sugar, pepper, remaining salt, and parsley. Toss lightly until butter is melted and beans are coated. Place in serving bowl; garnish with cherry tomatoes. *Yield about 6 servings.*

Fresh Green Beans

2   pounds fresh pole or bush beans
2   tablespoons peanut oil
1   cup Basic Chicken Stock (see Index)
1   tablespoon cornstarch
     Salt to taste

Cook beans in boiling water until crisp-tender; drain well. Heat oil in large skillet. Add beans; cook, stirring constantly, until heated through. Stir in stock; cover. Cook over high heat 3 minutes.

Blend cornstarch and 2 tablespoons water until smooth. Push beans to side of skillet; stir cornstarch mixture into broth. Stir beans into broth; cook, stirring constantly, until broth is slightly thickened and beans are glazed. Season with salt. Place beans in serving bowl. *Yield 6 to 8 servings.*

For a man seldom thinks with more earnestness of anything than he does of his dinner.

Hester Lynch Thrale (Piozzi) 1739–1821

Glazed Turnips

2   pounds white turnips, peeled and quartered
2   tablespoons vegetable oil
1   to 1½ cups beef bouillon
1   tablespoon butter or margarine
3   tablespoons sugar
2   tablespoons parsley, minced

Blanch turnips in boiling salted water to cover 5 minutes; drain. Pat dry with paper towels. Sauté in hot oil 3 minutes to brown lightly. Pour in just enough bouillon to cover. Add butter and sugar; cover. Boil slowly 20 to 30 minutes, until turnips are just tender. Uncover; boil liquid to reduce to thick syrup.

Gently top turnips; coat with glaze. Place in vegetable dish or around a roast; sprinkle with parsley. *Yield 6 servings.*

Acorn Squash with Sliced Apples

3   fresh acorn squash, cut in half and seeds
    removed
    Salt to taste
2   or 3 fresh tart apples
    Butter
6   tablespoons brown sugar
    Nutmeg to taste

Place squash, cut-side-down, in shallow greased baking dish; add ½ cup boiling water; cover. Bake in preheated 350°F oven 10 minutes. Remove from oven; remove cover. Turn squash cut-side-up; sprinkle with salt.

Peel and core apples; cut into wedges. Fill squash cavities with apples; dot generously with butter. Sprinkle each squash half with 1 tablespoon brown sugar, then with a little nutmeg. Pour ½ cup boiling water into baking dish. Bake 30 minutes, or until squash and apples are tender. *Yield 6 servings.*

Summer Squash in Cream

4   medium to small summer squash, peeled
    and seeds removed
    Salt and pepper
3   tablespoons butter or margarine
1   cup all-purpose cream
1   tablespoon parsley, chopped

Slice squash into a buttered, deep baking dish. Sprinkle with salt and pepper; dot with butter. Place in preheated 400°F oven; cover. When tender, add cream; cook, uncovered, until slightly browned. Sprinkle with parsley. Serve in cooking dish. *Yield 6 servings.*

Fried Zucchini

1   egg
1   tablespoon milk
3   tablespoons flour
1   teaspoon salt
1   teaspoon garlic salt
3   to 4 medium zucchini, washed and sliced
    into rounds about ¼ inch thick
    Deep fat for frying

Combine egg, milk, flour, salt, and garlic salt in bowl; mix well to form batter. Dip each zucchini round into batter; fry in deep fat. Batter zucchini when ready to fry, so each piece is coated; fry until crisp and golden brown. Drain on paper towels. Serve hot. *Yield 4 to 6 servings.*

Kissing don't last; cookery do!

George Meredith 1828–1909

Scalloped Zucchini

6   cups zucchini, thinly sliced
1   cup boiling water
¾   cup Basic White Sauce (see Index)
2   eggs, beaten
1   teaspoon salt
½   teaspoon Worcestershire sauce
1   teaspoon onion, finely chopped
¼   cup fine dry bread crumbs
1   tablespoon butter or margarine, melted

Cook zucchini in boiling water until tender, about 5 minutes; drain.

Make White Sauce. Stir a little into eggs; gradually stir eggs into remaining sauce. Stir in salt, Worcestershire sauce, onion, and squash. Put in greased 1-quart casserole.

Mix crumbs with butter; sprinkle over squash mixture. Bake in preheated 325°F oven about 35 minutes. *Yield 6 servings.*

No Swimming - 1921

Salads and Salad Dressings

Chef's Salad

½   head Boston lettuce, washed and torn into bite-sized pieces
1   large tomato, cut into eighths
½   cucumber, thinly sliced
1   small onion, grated
½   green pepper, cut into thin strips
½   cup plain yogurt
1   tablespoon lemon juice
½   teaspoon salt
⅛   teaspoon white pepper
1   clove garlic, minced
1   teaspoon parsley, chopped
1   teaspoon dried dill
½   cup cooked chicken, cut into julienne strips
½   cup cooked ham, chopped
¼   cup low-fat mozzarella cheese, cut into julienne strips
2   sardines, drained, cut in half lengthwise
3   stuffed green olives, sliced

Arrange lettuce on salad platter with tomato, cucumber, onion, and green pepper; cover. Refrigerate while preparing rest of ingredients and dressing.

Blend yogurt with lemon juice; season with salt, pepper, garlic, parsley, and dill. Pour dressing over salad greens; arrange meats, cheese, and sardines on top. Garnish with olives. *Yield 4 servings.*

The Breakfast Table - 1930

Chicken Salad with Bacon

1	small head iceberg lettuce, torn into large pieces
1	small red sweet pepper, cut in strips
1	cucumber, thickly sliced
1	cup small whole mushrooms
2	cups chicken, coarsely chopped
2	hard-boiled eggs, quartered
4	slices crisp-fried bacon, halved
2	tablespoons wine vinegar
6	tablespoons salad oil
	Salt to taste
¼	cup Roquefort cheese, mashed

Place lettuce in salad bowl. Add red pepper, cucumber, mushrooms, and chicken; toss lightly. Top with eggs and bacon.

Combine vinegar, oil, salt, and cheese and blend thoroughly. Serve with the salad. *Yield 4 servings.*

Home for Thanksgiving - 1945

Ho! 'tis the time of salads.

Laurence Sterne 1713–1768

Waldorf Salad

½	cup mayonnaise
½	cup sour cream
1	tablespoon honey
1½	cups tart apples, peeled, cored, and diced
1	cup celery, diced
½	cup walnuts, coarsely chopped
1	cup grapes, halved and seeded

Combine mayonnaise, sour cream, and honey. Add apples; mix well to prevent apple discoloring. Add celery, walnuts, and grapes; mix lightly. Chill well before serving. *Yield 3 to 4 servings.*

Fresh Crab Salad

1	pound fresh crab meat, flaked
½	cup celery, minced
1	teaspoon onion, grated
1	tablespoon pimiento, minced
¼	teaspoon salt
2	tablespoons lemon juice
	Mayonnaise
	Lettuce leaves
2	tablespoons parsley, minced

Combine crab meat, celery, onion, and pimiento in bowl. Sprinkle with salt and lemon juice; toss to mix. Add just enough mayonnaise to moisten; mix well. Spoon onto bed of lettuce; sprinkle with parsley.

Garnish with thin slices of cucumber and tomato. Serve with additional mayonnaise. *Yield 4 servings.*

A feast is made for laughter . . .

The Bible, Ecclesiastes

Mixed Green Salad

1   head Bibb lettuce (or ½ head iceberg lettuce), washed, dried, torn into bite-sized pieces
2   green peppers, cleaned, seeded, and cut into strips
4   small tomatoes, sliced
2   small onions, sliced and separated into rings
2   hard-cooked eggs, sliced
½   cup stuffed green olives, sliced
½   medium cucumber, peeled, seeded, and cut into chunks

Salad Dressing
4   tablespoons olive oil
3   tablespoons tarragon vinegar
½   teaspoon salt
¼   teaspoon freshly ground pepper
1   clove garlic, crushed
¼   teaspoon crushed oregano
1   tablespoon fresh parsley, chopped

Place lettuce in salad bowl. Add peppers, tomatoes, onions, eggs, olives, and cucumber; refrigerate.

Combine all dressing ingredients; mix well. At serving time toss salad at table with prepared dressing. *Yield 4 servings.*

Cole Slaw

1   head cabbage, very thinly sliced
1   cup mayonnaise
1   cup sour cream
1   teaspoon prepared mustard
1   tablespoon lemon juice
    Salt and pepper to taste
1   tablespoon sugar

Place cabbage in a bowl.

Mix other ingredients; stir into cabbage. Chill about 4 hours. *Yield 10 servings.*

Luncheon Egg Salad

2¼ cups Basic Mayonnaise (see Index)
1¼ cups chili sauce
¾   cup catsup
9   hard-cooked eggs, chopped
1½ cups celery, diced
½   cup green pepper, minced
1   teaspoon sugar
½   teaspoon Worcestershire sauce
    Salt and pepper to taste
3   tablespoons gelatin
¾   cup cold water
    Avocado and mandarin orange slices
4   tablespoons Vinaigrette (see below)

Combine first 9 ingredients. Soften gelatin in small amount of cold water. Place in small saucepan over low heat and dissolve, stirring constantly. Stir in egg mixture. Pour into ring mold and chill until firm.

Unmold on lettuce and fill center with avocado and orange slices mixed with Vinaigrette. Crab meat and shrimp may be added to egg mixture, if desired. *Yield 12 to 16 servings.*

He that is of a merry heart hath a continual feast.

The Bible, *Proverbs*

Vinaigrette

2   teaspoons salt
½   teaspoon freshly ground pepper
1   teaspoon prepared mustard
1   cup olive oil
¼   cup red-wine vinegar

Place salt, pepper, and mustard in medium-size bowl. Add several drops oil; blend with wooden spoon. Add several drops vinegar; blend well. Add remaining oil and vinegar gradually, stirring constantly, until all is used. Store in covered jar in refrigerator. Shake well before using. *Yield 1⅓ cups.*

French Dressing

2   tablespoons white-wine vinegar
     Salt
     Freshly ground black pepper
6   to 8 tablespoons olive oil and/or peanut oil

Mix vinegar with salt and pepper to taste. Add oil; beat with fork until mixture thickens.

Note: For slightly thicker dressing, add an ice cube; stir 1 to 2 minutes longer; remove ice. *Yield 1½ cups.*

Russian Dressing

1   cup mayonnaise
1   tablespoon chili sauce
1   to 2 teaspoons chopped chives
2   teaspoons red pepper or canned pimiento, chopped

Combine all ingredients. Serve with egg or vegetable salads or with fish. *Yield 1¼ cups.*

Note: Chili sauce varies considerably in strength. It is advisable to add about ½ teaspoon, then taste and increase quantity as necessary. Quantity given is for mild chili sauce.

Blue or Roquefort Cheese Dressing

4   ounces blue or Roquefort cheese, crumbled
1   cup sour cream
1   teaspoon lemon juice
1   teaspoon sugar
1   teaspoon instant minced onion
½   teaspoon salt

Mix all ingredients well. Chill, preferably overnight, to allow flavors to blend. Use within a week. *Yield about 1½ cups.*

I like nothing better than to go out in the country and bloviate.

Warren Gamaliel Harding 1920

Breads and Muffins

Old-Fashioned Biscuits

2   cups flour
1   tablespoon baking powder
1   teaspoon salt
⅓   cup shortening
    About ¾ cup milk

Mix dry ingredients thoroughly. Mix in shortening only until mixture is crumbly. Add most of milk; stir to mix. Add more milk as needed to make dough that is soft but not too sticky to knead.

Knead dough gently on lightly floured surface 10 to 12 times. Form into ball. Pat or roll dough to ½ to ¾ inch thick. Cut with floured biscuit cutter or cut into squares with knife. Place on ungreased baking sheet 1 inch apart for crusty biscuits, close together for softer biscuits.

Bake at 450°F 12 to 15 minutes, until golden brown. *Yield 12 biscuits.*

Sour Milk Biscuits

3   cups all-purpose flour
4   teaspoons baking powder
    Pinch of soda
1   teaspoon salt
½   cup vegetable shortening
1½ cups sour milk or buttermilk
    Melted butter

Sift flour, baking powder, soda, and salt together in large bowl. Cut in shortening with 2 knives or pastry blender to make a coarse, crumb-like consistency. Add milk, blending well.

Place dough on lightly floured surface and knead until smooth. Roll out to ½-inch thickness and cut into rounds with a biscuit cutter. Place on greased baking sheet and brush with melted butter. Bake in preheated 450°F oven for 12 to 15 minutes, or until golden brown. *Yield about 2 dozen biscuits.*

Maryland Beaten Biscuits

5   cups all-purpose flour
2   teaspoons salt
½   teaspoon baking powder
1   cup lard

Combine flour, salt, and baking powder in mixing bowl. Cut in lard to make a fine crumb-like consistency. Add enough water to make a stiff dough, then knead until dough holds together. Place on heavy table or chopping block. Beat with a hammer for 30 minutes, or until the dough is blistered.

Shape into small biscuits and place on baking sheet, then prick tops with fork. Bake in preheated 400°F oven for about 15 minutes, or until lightly browned. *Yield 35 to 40 biscuits.*

The one them said to his make,
"Where shall we our breakfast
take?"

                                                        Anonymous

Popovers

1   cup flour
¼   teaspoon salt
2   eggs, beaten
1   cup milk (scant measure)
1   tablespoon shortening, melted

Preheat oven to 450°F. Sift flour and salt together. Mix eggs, milk, and shortening; add gradually to flour. Beat until smooth, with egg whisk or electric mixer, about 1 minute. Pour into greased popover tins, Pyrex cups, or muffin pans to ⅓ full.

Bake 20 minutes. Reduce heat to 350°F; bake 15 minutes, until popovers are firm. *Yield about 8 large popovers.*

Cornbread

1   cup cornmeal
1   cup flour
1   tablespoon baking powder
½   teaspoon salt
2   to 4 tablespoons sugar (optional)
1   egg
1   cup milk
¼   cup melted fat or oil

Mix cornmeal, flour, baking powder, salt, and sugar. Set aside. Beat egg. Add milk. Add fat. Add to cornmeal mixture; stir just enough to mix. Fill greased 9 × 9-inch pan half full.

Bake at 425°F 20 to 25 minutes, until lightly browned. *Yield 6 servings.*

Blueberry Muffins

½   cup butter
1   cup sugar
2   eggs
2   cups flour
2   teaspoons baking powder
½   teaspoon salt
½   cup milk
2   cups fresh or frozen blueberries
1   teaspoon vanilla
2   teaspoons sugar

On low speed of electric mixer, cream butter and 1 cup of the sugar until fluffy. Add eggs, one at a time, and mix until blended. Sift flour, baking powder, and salt together. Mix dry ingredients with butter mixture alternately with milk. Add blueberries and vanilla.

Grease a muffin tin, including the top of the muffin tin, or you can use paper-cup cake liners. Pile batter high in tins and sprinkle with remaining 2 teaspoons of sugar. Bake at 375°F for 30 minutes. *Yield 12 muffins.*

Springtime

Cornmeal Muffins

½ cup cornmeal
½ cup all-purpose flour
2 tablespoons sugar
½ teaspoon salt
2 teaspoons baking powder
1 egg, beaten
½ cup milk
2 tablespoons bacon drippings

Sift cornmeal, flour, sugar, salt, and baking powder together into mixing bowl. Stir in egg, milk, and bacon drippings, mixing well.

Fill 8 greased muffin cups ⅔ full with batter. Bake in preheated 425°F oven for 15 minutes, or until browned. *Yield 8 muffins.*

Orange Muffins

2 cups all-purpose flour, sifted
1 teaspoon soda
1 teaspoon salt
½ cup vegetable shortening
    Grated rind of 1 orange
1 square unsweetened chocolate, grated
1½ cups (about) buttermilk

Sift flour, soda, and salt together into bowl. Cut in shortening until mixture is consistency of cornmeal. Add grated rind and chocolate, then stir in enough buttermilk to make a soft dough.

Place on floured board and knead lightly. Roll out ½ inch thick and cut with a floured round cutter the size of the muffin cups; place in greased muffin cups.

Bake in preheated 475°F oven for about 15 minutes. *Yield about 12 muffins.*

English Muffins

1   cup milk, scalded
2   tablespoons sugar
1   teaspoon salt
¼   cup butter
2   packages dry yeast
1   cup warm water
5½   cups (about) all-purpose flour
     Cornmeal

Combine hot milk, sugar, salt, and butter, stirring until sugar is dissolved and butter is melted. Place in large mixing bowl and cool to lukewarm. Dissolve yeast in warm water, stirring well, then add to milk mixture. Beat in 3 cups of flour until smooth, then add enough of the remaining flour to make a soft dough.

Place dough on lightly floured surface and knead for about 8 to 10 minutes, or until smooth and elastic. Place dough in greased bowl, turning to grease the top. Cover and let the dough rise in a warm place for 1 hour, or until doubled in bulk. Punch down and divide in half.

Roll each dough section out to ½-inch thickness on a cornmeal-covered surface. Cut into circles with a 3-inch cookie cutter. Cover circles with towel and let rest for 30 minutes. Place circles, cornmeal sides down, in greased skillet over medium heat. Cook for about 15 minutes, or until bottoms are well browned. Turn over and cook other side for about 15 minutes longer, or until brown. *Yield about 20 muffins.*

Here is bread, which strengthens man's heart, and therefore called the staff of life.

Mathew Henry 1662–1714

My Reward - 1934

Spiced Rye Loaves

3   envelopes dry yeast
¼   cup melted butter
2½   cups lukewarm milk or water
2   teaspoons salt
6   tablespoons dark molasses or corn syrup
1   tablespoon wine vinegar
2   tablespoons caraway seed
4   cups rye flour
4   cups all-purpose flour

Place yeast in large mixing bowl. Mix butter, milk, and salt; then pour over the yeast and stir until yeast is dissolved. Add molasses, vinegar, and caraway seed and mix until blended. Add rye flour and half the all-purpose flour and mix well. Add enough of remaining all-purpose flour to make a stiff dough; mix until smooth. Cover and let rise until doubled in bulk.

Bake in preheated 325°F oven for about 1 hour, or until bread sounds hollow when tapped with fingers; then brush with water. Remove loaves from pans and cool on wire racks. One tablespoon aniseed or grated orange rind may be substituted for caraway seed. *Yield 2 loaves.*

Home-Baked White Bread

1½ cups lukewarm water
2   packages yeast
7½ cups all-purpose flour
3   tablespoons sugar
1   cup milk
1   tablespoon salt
¼   cup butter
1   recipe Anglais Glaze (see below)

Place water in large warm bowl or crock. Sprinkle yeast over water; stir until dissolved. Cover; let stand 15 minutes.

Combine 1½ cups flour and 2 tablespoons sugar. Beat mixture carefully into yeast mixture with wooden spoon until free from lumps. Cover with towel; let rise in warm place 30 minutes.

Scald milk; stir in salt and remaining sugar. Add butter; stir until dissolved. Cool to lukewarm. Add to yeast mixture. Add enough remaining flour to make soft dough.

Turn onto lightly floured board. Knead 10 minutes or until smooth and elastic; add flour if needed. Place in greased bowl; turn dough to grease top. Cover with towel; let rise in warm place 1 hour or until doubled in bulk.

Turn dough onto lightly floured board; divide in half. Shape into loaves. Place in 2 well-greased 9 × 5-inch loaf pans or 3 smaller shaped molds. Cover; let rise 1 hour or until doubled in bulk.

Bake at 400°F 10 minutes. Brush tops with Anglais Glaze, using pastry brush. Bake 15 minutes. Turn loaves onto wire racks to cool. *Yield 2 (9 × 5-inch) loaves.*

Anglais Glaze

1   egg
1   teaspoon vegetable oil
½   teaspoon salt
¼   teaspoon white pepper

Combine all ingredients; beat well. Strain before using.

Grandma's Whole-Wheat Bread

¾   cup milk
¼   cup brown sugar, firmly packed
1   tablespoon salt
⅓   cup butter
⅓   cup molasses
1½ cups lukewarm water
2   packages yeast
6   cups stone-ground, whole-wheat flour
1½ cups flour
1   recipe Egg Wash (see below)

Scald milk in small saucepan. Add brown sugar, salt, butter, and molasses. Stir until dissolved; let stand until lukewarm.

Pour water into warm, large mixing bowl. Sprinkle yeast over water, stirring until dissolved. Pour in milk mixture, stirring constantly. Stir in 4 cups whole-wheat flour, 1 cup at a time, mixing until smooth. Stir in remaining whole-wheat flour. Sprinkle with part of regular flour.

Turn dough onto floured surface. Knead in remaining flour about 10 minutes, or until dough is smooth and elastic. Place dough into well-buttered bowl; turn to grease top. Cover with towel; let rise in warm place 1 hour or until doubled in bulk.

Turn dough onto lightly floured surface; divide in half. Shape into loaves. Place in 2 well-greased 9 × 5-inch loaf pans. Cover; let rise in warm place about 1 hour or until doubled in bulk.

Bake at 400°F 10 minutes. Brush with Egg Wash; bake 15 minutes. *Yield 2 loaves.*

Egg Wash

1   egg white
1   teaspoon salt

Combine egg white and salt; beat with fork until foamy.

For a hot,
nourishing meal

Farmer's Fresh Potato Bread

1½ cups fresh potatoes, cubed
⅔   cup scalded milk
½   cup vegetable shortening
¼   cup sugar
2   teaspoons salt
2   packages dry yeast
3   large eggs, lightly beaten
8½ cups (about) all-purpose flour, sifted
3   tablespoons butter, melted

Place potatoes in small saucepan and add enough water to cover. Bring to a boil, then reduce heat and simmer until potatoes are tender. Drain potatoes, then mash. Measure 1 cup mashed potatoes and place in large bowl. Add milk, shortening, sugar, and salt and mix well. Cool to lukewarm.

Add yeast to ½ cup of warm water and stir until dissolved. Add to potato mixture, then add eggs and mix well. Add 1½ cups of flour and stir until well combined. Cover and let rise in a warm place for about 30 minutes, or until bubbly.

Stir in 5 cups of flour, 1 cup at a time, mixing well after each addition. Spread ½ cup of flour on a board. Place dough on the flour, then sprinkle 2 cups of flour over dough. Knead for 10 minutes, adding remaining flour as needed. Place dough in lightly greased bowl, turning to grease the surface; cover. Place in refrigerator overnight.

Divide dough in half and place in 2 greased loaf pans; then brush with butter. Let rise until doubled in bulk and bake at 350°F for about 40 minutes, or until brown. *Yield 2 loaves.*

I won't quarrel with my bread and butter.

Jonathan Swift 1667–1745

Nature's Friend - 1923

Yankee Spoon Bread

1   (10-ounce) package frozen kernel corn
3   cups milk
1   cup cornmeal
2   tablespoons plus 2 teaspoons butter
    Salt
1   teaspoon baking powder
3   eggs, separated

Preheat oven to 325°F. Cook corn according to directions. Drain; cool. Heat 2 cups milk.

Mix cornmeal with remaining cup of milk; add to hot milk. Cook until thick, stirring constantly. Add butter and salt; let cool. Add corn, baking powder, and slightly beaten egg yolks, mixing well.

Beat egg whites until stiff; fold into cornmeal mixture. Pour all into casserole. Bake about 45 minutes. *Yield 6 to 8 servings.*

Old-fashioned Breakfast - 1927

Old Country Caraway Rye Loaf

1   cake compressed yeast or 1 package active dry yeast
2   cups warm water
½   cup Sourdough Starter (see below)
2   cups all-purpose unbleached white flour
¼   cup molasses
1   teaspoon salt
3   tablespoons shortening, melted
2   tablespoons caraway seeds
4   to 4½ cups rye flour
¼   cup cornmeal
1   egg, beaten

Dissolve yeast in water. Add Sourdough Starter; blend thoroughly. Mix in white flour; cover. Set in warm place 12 hours or overnight.

Stir mixture to dissolve crust on top. Add molasses, salt, shortening, and caraway seeds; mix well. Add rye flour until soft dough has formed.

Pour 1 cup rye flour on kneading surface. Pour dough on flour. Knead flour into dough. Add enough remaining flour to form medium-stiff dough. Knead 10 minutes, or until folds form in dough.

Place dough ball in greased bowl. Grease top; cover. Let rise until doubled in bulk. Punch down dough. Knead 2 minutes. Form into oblong loaf. Place loaf on greased cookie sheet that has been dusted with cornmeal; cover. Let rise until doubled in bulk.

Place loaf in 400°F oven 10 minutes. Remove from oven. Brush with beaten egg. Return to oven. Bake 35 to 40 minutes, or until done. Cool on rack. *Yield 1 oblong loaf.*

Sourdough Starter

2   cups warm water
2   cups all-purpose white flour

Using stone jar or crock, combine water and flour. Place mixture in warm place 3 to 4 days, until bubbly and sour smelling. Refrigerate starter.

Each time it is used, replenish with equal parts water and flour; mix well. Cover; refrigerate. Starter will be ready when you next bake. Never use all your sourdough starter in a recipe. Reserve enough to keep it going. *Yield 2½ cups.*

Sweeter also than honey and the honeycomb.

The Bible, Psalms

Norman Rockwell

Desserts

Apple Cake

4   to 6 medium-size, tart apples, peeled, halved, and cored
2   lemons, juiced
3   tablespoons sugar
3   tablespoons butter
¾   cup sugar
2   egg yolks (do not put 2 yolks together; they will be used individually)
½   lemon, juiced and peel grated
1   teaspoon baking powder
1½ cups flour
¾   cup milk
1   tablespoon rum
2   egg whites
1   teaspoon butter (to grease pan)
1   teaspoon vegetable oil
3   tablespoons confectioners' sugar

Cut decorative lengthwise slits in apples, about ½ inch deep. Sprinkle with lemon juice and 3 tablespoons sugar; set aside.

Cream butter and ¾ cup sugar together. Beat in egg yolks one at a time. Gradually beat in lemon juice and grated peel.

Sift baking powder and flour together; gradually add to batter. Blend in milk and rum. In a small bowl, beat egg whites until stiff; fold into batter.

Generously grease springform pan. Pour in batter; top with apple halves. Brush apples with oil. Bake in preheated 350°F oven 35 to 40 minutes. Remove from pan; sprinkle with confectioners' sugar. *Yield 6 servings.*

Basic Chocolate Cake

½   cup butter or margarine
2   cups sugar
3   eggs
1½ teaspoons vanilla
3   squares unsweetened chocolate, melted and cooled
2   cups cake flour, sifted
2   teaspoons baking soda
½   teaspoon salt
1   cup sour cream
1   cup boiling water

Beat butter and sugar together in large bowl. Add eggs; beat until light and fluffy. Beat in vanilla and chocolate.

Sift dry ingredients together. Add alternately with sour cream to butter mixture; beat well after each addition. Stir in boiling water. (Batter will be thin.) Pour into 2 greased and floured 9-inch layer-cake pans.

Bake in preheated 350°F oven 35 minutes, or until cake tests done. Cool in pan on wire racks 10 minutes. Turn out onto racks; cool completely. Fill and frost as desired. *Yield 12 servings.*

The proof of the pudding is in the eating.

Miguel de Cervantes 1547–1616

Chilled Cheesecake

3   tablespoons butter, melted
¾   cup graham-cracker crumbs
     Sugar
¼   teaspoon cinnamon
¼   teaspoon nutmeg
2   envelopes unflavored gelatin
2   eggs, separated
1   cup milk
1   teaspoon lemon rind, grated
1   tablespoon lemon juice
1   teaspoon vanilla extract
3   cups creamed cottage cheese
1   cup whipping cream, whipped

Combine butter, graham-cracker crumbs, 2 tablespoons of sugar, cinnamon, and nutmeg in bowl. Press ½ cup of crumb mixture into 8- or 9-inch springform pan.

Combine gelatin and ¾ cup sugar in medium saucepan. Beat egg yolks, then stir in milk gradually. Stir into gelatin mixture and place over low heat. Cook, stirring constantly, for 3 to 5 minutes, or until gelatin dissolves and mixture is slightly thickened. Remove from heat and stir in lemon rind, lemon juice, and vanilla extract.

Beat cottage cheese with electric mixer at high speed for 3 to 4 minutes, or until smooth. Stir into gelatin mixture, then chill, stirring occasionally, until mixture mounds slightly when dropped from spoon.

Beat egg whites until stiff but not dry. Add ¼ cup sugar gradually and beat until very stiff. Fold into gelatin mixture, then fold in the whipped cream. Turn into prepared pan and sprinkle with remaining crumb mixture. Chill for 3 to 4 hours, or until firm. Loosen side of pan with a sharp knife and release springform.

An 8-cup loaf pan may be used instead of springform pan. Grease loaf pan lightly. Cut waxed paper to fit pan and line loaf pan. Invert onto serving plate to unmold, then remove waxed paper. *Yield 12 servings.*

Basic Yellow Cake

¾   cup butter or margarine, softened
1⅔   cups sugar
2   eggs
2   teaspoons vanilla
3   cups cake flour, sifted
2½   teaspoons baking powder
½   teaspoon salt
1⅓   cups milk

Beat butter, sugar, eggs, and vanilla in large bowl.

Sift dry ingredients together. Add alternately with milk to butter mixture; beat until smooth after addition. Pour into 2 greased and floured 9-inch layer-cake pans.

Bake in preheated 350°F oven 30 minutes, or until cake tests done. Cool in pans on wire racks 10 minutes. Turn out onto racks; cool completely. Fill and frost as desired. *Yield 12 servings.*

Cleaning Up - 1959

Fresh Coconut Cake

1   cup shortening
2   cups sugar
1   teaspoon vanilla extract
3   cups cake flour, sifted
3   teaspoons baking powder
1   teaspoon salt
½   cup milk
½   cup coconut milk
1   cup coconut, freshly grated
6   egg whites, stiffly beaten

Fresh Coconut Icing
1   cup plus 1 teaspoon sugar
¼   cup coconut milk
¼   teaspoon salt
½   teaspoon cream of tartar
2   egg whites
3   tablespoons water
1   teaspoon vanilla extract
2   cups coconut, freshly grated

Cream shortening and sugar together in large mixer bowl, then add vanilla extract. Sift flour, baking powder, and salt together. Add to creamed mixture alternately with milk and coconut milk, beating well after each addition. Stir in 1 cup coconut, then fold in egg whites carefully but thoroughly. Turn into 2 greased and floured 9-inch layer-cake pans with removable bottoms.

Bake in preheated 375°F oven for 30 minutes, or until cake tests done. Cool in pans for 10 minutes, then turn out on wire racks to cool completely.

Make icing. Stir 1 teaspoon sugar into the coconut milk, then spoon over the cake layers. Combine 1 cup sugar, salt, cream of tartar, egg whites, 3 tablespoons water, and vanilla extract in top of double boiler and stir until blended. Place over boiling water and cook for 7 minutes, beating constantly at high speed with an electric hand mixer. Stir in 1 cup coconut.

Frost between layers and over top and side of cake. Sprinkle half the remaining coconut over top of cake, then press remaining coconut lightly around side of cake. *Yield 12 servings.*

Gingerbread

½   cup butter or margarine
½   cup brown sugar, firmly packed
1   egg
½   cup molasses
1½ cups flour
½   teaspoon salt
¾   teaspoon baking soda
½   teaspoon ginger
½   teaspoon cinnamon
½   cup boiling water

Beat butter and sugar until creamy. Add egg and molasses; beat well.

Mix dry ingredients thoroughly. Add to molasses mixture alternately with boiling water. Beat after each addition. Pour into greased 8×8×2-inch baking pan.

Bake at 350°F 35 to 40 minutes. Serve warm. *Yield 6 to 9 servings.*

Butter-Cream Frosting

½   cup butter
4   cups confectioners' sugar, sifted
1   egg
⅛   teaspoon salt
1   teaspoon vanilla extract
2   tablespoons light cream

Cream butter until light and fluffy. Gradually add half the sugar; beat well after each addition. Blend in egg, salt, and vanilla. Add remaining sugar alternately with cream; beat until smooth after each addition. *Yield 2½ cups; enough for 2 (9-inch) layers.*

Marshmallow Icing

1   cup sugar
⅓   cup water
2   egg whites, stiffly beaten
⅓   teaspoon cream of tartar
1½ teaspoons vanilla

Boil sugar and water; add slowly to egg whites. While still warm, add cream of tartar and vanilla; beat until bowl is cool. *Yield enough for 2 (9-inch) layers.*

Grandma's Kitchen - 1938

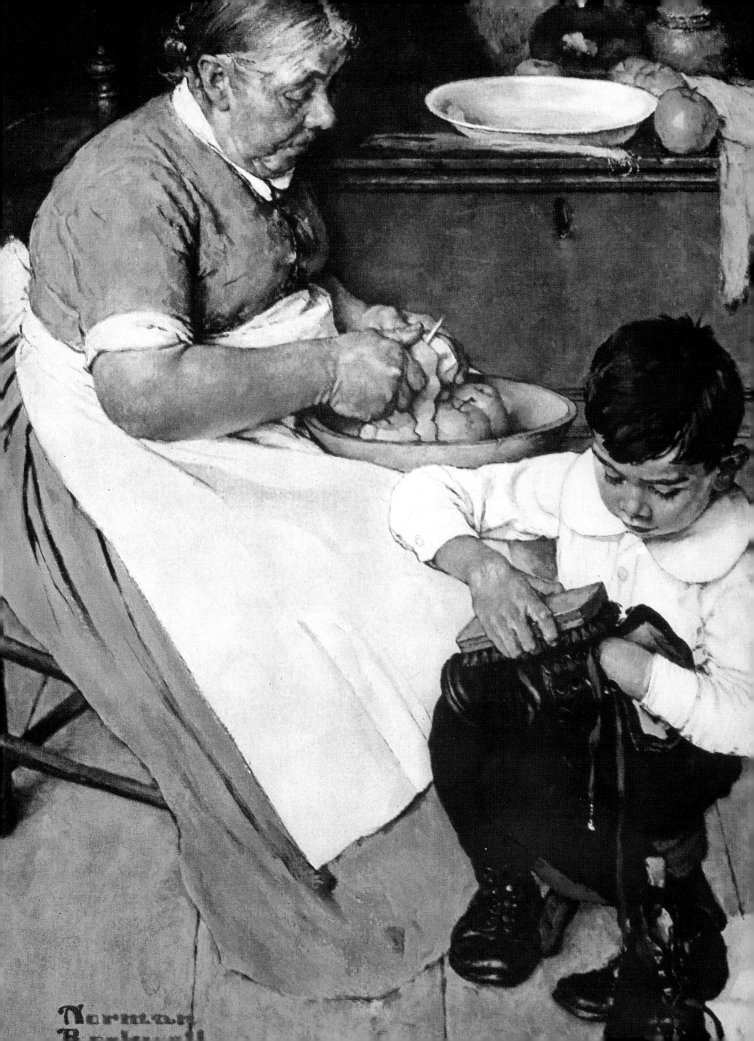

Creamy Chocolate Frosting

2   squares (2 ounces) unsweetened baking
    chocolate
½   cup milk
1½ cups sugar
2   egg yolks, beaten
1   tablespoon butter
1   teaspoon vanilla extract

Put chocolate and milk into pan; stir over low heat until chocolate has melted.

Mix sugar with egg yolks; add to chocolate mixture. Cook gently 10 minutes, stirring frequently. Add butter and vanilla; leave until lukewarm. Beat until thick enough to spread. *Yield enough for 2 (9-inch) layers.*

Apple Cobbler

4   cups baking apples, peeled and sliced
1⅓ cups sugar
⅛   teaspoon cinnamon
½   teaspoon almond extract (optional)
2   tablespoons butter
1½ cups flour, sifted
2   teaspoons baking powder
½   teaspoon salt
¼   cup butter
1   egg, beaten
⅔   cup milk

Place apples in 1½-quart baking dish. Sprinkle with 1 cup sugar, cinnamon, and almond extract; dot with 2 tablespoons butter.

Sift flour, baking powder, ⅓ cup sugar, and salt into mixing bowl. Cut in ¼ cup butter until mixture is slightly coarser than cornmeal.

Combine egg and milk; pour into dry ingredients. Stir just enough to combine; spoon over apples in baking dish.

Bake in 425°F oven about 30 minutes, until browned. Serve with fresh cream, sour cream, or ice cream, if desired. *Yield 6 to 8 servings.*

Apple Fritters

4   to 6 cooking apples, peeled and cored
    White wine to cover

Fritter Batter
2   egg yolks
⅔   cup milk
1   tablespoon lemon juice
1   tablespoon butter, melted
1   cup flour
¼   teaspoon salt
2   tablespoons sugar
2   egg whites, beaten stiff

   Deep fat for frying

Cut apples crosswise into ½-inch slices. Each slice will have a hole in center. Soak slices in wine 2 hours.

Combine batter ingredients in order given by stirring with wooden spoon. Fold in egg whites last.

Drain apples; drop one at a time in fritter batter. Heat fat in large skillet. Fry apple fritters until lightly browned all over; drain on paper towel. Serve piping hot. *Yield 4 to 6 servings.*

Apple Crunch

3   medium apples, pared and sliced
¼   cup brown sugar, firmly packed
¾   cup flour
¾   cup white sugar
¼   teaspoon salt
¼   teaspoon cinnamon
1   egg
⅓   cup margarine or butter, melted

Mix apples with brown sugar in baking pan; set aside. Mix flour, sugar, salt, and cinnamon; set aside. Beat egg; mix with flour mixture. Spread over fruit. Pour margarine over top.

Bake at 375°F about 45 minutes, until lightly browned. Serve warm. *Yield 6 servings.*

Peach Dumplings

1¾ **cups flour, unsifted**
1   **teaspoon salt**
½   **cup butter or margarine**
1   **egg yolk**
3   **tablespoons water**
1   **tablespoon lemon juice**
2   **tablespoons sugar**
½   **teaspoon cinnamon**
6   **peach halves, fresh or canned, drained**
¾   **cup sugar and ⅔ cup water***

Mix flour and salt thoroughly. Mix in butter with pastry blender or fork. Mix egg yolks, 3 tablespoons water, and lemon juice together. Mix lightly into flour mixture with fork. Roll dough on lightly floured surface into 12 × 18-inch rectangle. Cut into 6 (6-inch) squares.

Mix 2 tablespoons sugar and cinnamon. Roll peach halves in sugar mixture. Place peach half, hollow-side-down, in center of each pastry square. Bring corners together over peach. Moisten; seal. Place in greased 8 × 8 × 2-inch baking pan; allow space between dumplings.

Heat ¾ cup sugar and water to boiling. Pour over dumplings. Bake in preheated 425°F oven about 40 minutes, until browned. *Yield 6 servings.*

* Three-fourths cup syrup drained from canned peaches can be used in place of sugar and water. Heat to boiling before pouring over dumplings.

Cherries Jubilee

3   **tablespoons red currant jelly**
1   **tablespoon butter**
½   **cup kirsch, heated**
2   **cups canned tart cherries, well drained**
1   **pint vanilla ice cream**

Melt jelly in frying pan or chafing dish. Add butter; stir until melted and hot. Add cherries; heat through.

Pour kirsch over cherries; ignite with long match. Let burn until flames die. Spoon hot cherries over ice cream; serve. *Yield 4 servings.*

Birthday Party - 1952

Basic Pastry

1   cup all-purpose flour
½   teaspoon salt
⅓   cup shortening
2   tablespoons water

Sift flour and salt into bowl. Cut in shortening with pastry blender until particles are size of peas. Sprinkle with water, 1 teaspoon at a time; mix lightly with fork. Gather dough together with fingers; press into ball. Refrigerate until required. *Yield one 8- or 9-inch pie crust.*

Note: If pie shell is to be baked without a filling, line pie plate with pastry; prick bottom with fork or put piece of greased paper (greased-side-down) in bottom. Fill with rice, beans, or crusts of bread. (These can then be stored for future use.) Remove paper and beans a few minutes before end of cooking.

Royal Short Pastry

2   cups all-purpose flour
1   teaspoon salt
¼   cup vegetable shortening
1   teaspoon vinegar
1   egg
1   to 2 tablespoons water

Sift flour and salt together into bowl. Add shortening and blend with pastry blender until mixture resembles meal. Add vinegar and egg and mix. Add water, a tablespoon at a time, until ingredients hold together.

Roll out pastry on floured surface to fit two 9-inch pie pans. Place in pans and crimp or flute edges. Prick sides and bottoms well with fork. Bake in preheated, 400°F oven for 15 to 17 minutes or until lightly browned. *Yield two 9-inch pie crusts.*

*The best of all physicians
Is Apple-pie and cheese!*

Eugene Field 1850–1895

Never-Fail Short Pastry

1   cup vegetable shortening
½   cup boiling water
1   teaspoon salt
3   cups all-purpose flour, sifted

Cream shortening with boiling water until well mixed, either by hand or with electric mixer. Add salt and flour all at once and stir until thoroughly mixed. Form into ball; chill in covered container for at least an hour.

Roll out half the dough for a single shell. Fit into pie pan; then prick generously with fork around edges and on bottom. Bake at 450°F for 15 minutes for a single crust. Dough may be kept for at least 3 weeks in refrigerator. *Yield two 9-inch pie crusts.*

Classic Apple Pie

1   recipe Royal Short Pastry or Never-Fail Short Pastry (see Index)
¾   cup sugar
1   tablespoon all-purpose flour
½   teaspoon ground cinnamon
¼   teaspoon ground nutmeg
⅛   teaspoon salt
1   tablespoon lemon rind, grated
5   cups Washington State apple slices
1   tablespoon lemon juice
2   tablespoons butter or margarine

Roll out half the pastry and line a 9-inch pie plate.

Combine sugar, flour, cinnamon, nutmeg, salt, and lemon rind in bowl. Add apples and toss to coat evenly. Arrange apples in pastry-lined pie plate. Sprinkle with lemon juice and dot with butter.

Roll out remaining pastry and place over apples. Cut air vents in top. Trim pastry and flute edge, trimming excess pastry. Bake in preheated 425°F oven 40 to 45 minutes, or until crust is golden brown. *Yield 6 to 8 servings.*

Blueberry Pie

4   cups fresh blueberries, rinsed and drained
¾   cup sugar
     Juice of 1 lemon
1⅔ cups flour
2   teaspoons sugar
     Dash of salt
1   cup vegetable shortening
4   tablespoons ice water

Sprinkle blueberries with ¾ cup sugar; squeeze lemon juice over top. Set aside.

Sift flour, 2 teaspoons sugar, and salt into mixing bowl. Cut shortening into flour. Gradually add ice water; mix with pastry blender. Chill dough.

Divide dough into 2 parts. Roll out half on floured board until thin enough to cover sides and bottom of 9-inch pie plate. Prick bottom with fork. Bake bottom crust 10 minutes at 400°F. This prevents berry juice from soaking through crust. Cool bottom crust about 10 minutes while rolling out remaining dough and cutting into strips.

Fill bottom shell with blueberries; place strips of dough across top for latticework effect. Use 1 or 2 long strips around edge of plate to seal crusts. Bake no longer than 20 minutes at 400°F. If desired, top crust can be rolled into 1 piece and used to make a 2-crust pie. *Yield 6 to 8 servings.*

Sweet Georgia Peach Pie

1   unbaked pie shell (see Index: Basic Pastry)
6   to 8 large fresh peaches, peeled and sliced
4   eggs
1   cup sugar
2   tablespoons flour
2   tablespoons shortening, melted

Prepare pie shell; fill with peaches.

Beat eggs well in bowl; add sugar, flour, and shortening. Pour over peaches. It will form its own top crust in baking. Bake at 400°F 15 minutes. Lower oven to 325°F; cook 40 minutes more. Let cool to room temperature. Slice; serve. *Yield 6 to 8 servings.*

Boston Cream Pie

Cake
⅓   cup butter or margarine
1   cup sugar
2   eggs
1   teaspoon vanilla
1¼ cups all-purpose flour, unsifted
1½ teaspoons baking powder
¼   teaspoon salt
¾   cup milk

Filling
⅓   cup sugar
2   tablespoons cornstarch
1½ cups milk
2   egg yolks, slightly beaten
1   tablespoon butter
1   teaspoon vanilla

Glaze
3   tablespoons water
2   tablespoons butter
3   tablespoons cocoa
1   cup confectioners' sugar
½   teaspoon vanilla

Cream butter, sugar, eggs, and vanilla in medium bowl until light and fluffy.

Combine dry ingredients; add alternately with milk to creamed mixture. Pour batter into well-greased and floured 9-inch layer pan. Bake in preheated 350°F oven 30 to 35 minutes or until cake tester inserted in center comes out clean. Cool 10 minutes; remove from pan. Cool completely on rack. Cut into 2 thin layers.

Make filling. Combine sugar, cornstarch, milk, and egg yolks in saucepan. Cook and stir over medium heat until mixture boils; boil and stir 1 minute. Remove from heat; blend in butter and vanilla. Cover; chill. Spread filling onto 1 cake layer; top with remaining cake layer.

Make glaze. Combine water and butter in small saucepan; bring to full boil. Remove from heat; immediately stir in cocoa. Beat in sugar and vanilla (whisk if necessary) until smooth; cool slightly. Pour glaze on top of cake; let some drizzle down sides. Chill before serving. *Yield 6 servings.*

Pecan Pie

1   (9- or 11-inch) unbaked pie shell (see
     Index: Basic Pastry)
5   eggs
¾   cup sugar
1½   cups dark syrup
1½   cups pecans, chopped or halved
¾   teaspoon salt
2   teaspoons vanilla
     Whipped cream (for decoration)

Prepare pie shell; set aside.

Beat eggs slightly in large bowl. Add sugar, syrup, nuts, salt, and vanilla; mix until nicely blended. Pour into pie shell. Bake at 325°F 50 minutes. When cool, garnish with whipped cream; serve at once. *Yield 6 to 8 servings.*

Lemon Sherbet

1½   teaspoons unflavored gelatin
2   tablespoons cold water
2   cups skim milk
¾   cup sugar
½   cup lemon juice
½   teaspoon lemon rind, grated
2   egg whites, stiffly beaten

Soak gelatin in water several minutes.

Heat milk. Add sugar and gelatin; stir until dissolved. Chill in refrigerator until just starting to become firm. Gradually stir in lemon juice and rind. Pour into freezing tray; freeze to a mush.

Turn into chilled bowl; beat with electric beater until fluffy but not melted. Fold in egg whites. Return to freezer; freeze until firm. *Yield 6 servings.*

Basic Egg Custard

2   eggs
2   egg yolks
½   cup sugar
3   cups milk
1   teaspoon vanilla extract

Beat eggs, egg yolks, and sugar together using an electric mixer at medium speed, for about 5 minutes or until thick and doubled in bulk. Heat milk and vanilla in heavy saucepan slowly until hot, but not boiling.

Stir milk into egg mixture. Pour into top of large double boiler. Cook over hot water, stirring constantly, for about 20 minutes or until thickened. *Yield about 3 cups thin custard, which may also be used as a sauce.*

Begging - 1925

Ice-Cream Pie

2   large chocolate bars
⅔   cup water
2   heaping teaspoons instant coffee
1   (9-inch) baked pie shell
½   gallon vanilla ice cream, softened
1   small chocolate bar, shaved

In saucepan, melt 2 large chocolate bars with water. Add instant coffee. Pour into pie shell; let cool. Fill with ice cream; top with chocolate shavings. Place in freezer; serve frozen. *Yield 8 servings.*

Butterscotch Bread Pudding

3   tablespoons butter or margarine
½   cup brown sugar
¼   teaspoon baking soda
2   cups milk
2   eggs
     Pinch of salt
2   cups stale bread cubes (about ½-inch cubes)

Melt butter in pan. Add sugar; heat until well blended. Dissolve soda in milk; add gradually to sugar mixture. Stir until well blended; set aside to cool.

Beat eggs lightly. Add salt and cooled milk-and-sugar mixture.

Put bread cubes into greased baking dish; pour custard over. Bake in preheated 350°F oven about 45 minutes. *Yield 6 servings.*

Hard Sauce

1   cup butter, softened
1   (1-pound) box confectioners' sugar, sifted
¼   cup brandy

Cream butter with electric mixer until light. Add sugar gradually; beat until fluffy. Add brandy; blend well. Serve immediately. Store any remaining sauce in refrigerator. Bring to room temperature before serving. *Yield about 3 cups.*

Steamed Chocolate Pudding

½   cup butter, softened
¾   cup sugar
¾   cup all-purpose flour
3   tablespoons cocoa
⅛   teaspoon salt
3   eggs
½   teaspoon vanilla extract
¼   cup half-and-half cream
     Confectioners' sugar

Cream butter in mixing bowl with electric mixer until light and fluffy. Add sugar; beat for about 5 minutes. Sift flour, cocoa, and salt together. Beat in flour mixture and eggs alternately, beginning and ending with flour mixture. Add vanilla extract and cream; beat in thoroughly.

Turn into very heavily buttered 1- to 1½-quart metal mold or pyrex dish: use 1 to 2 tablespoons butter to grease mold. Place a double thickness of buttered waxed paper over top, then cover with a double thickness of heavy-duty foil. Tie this tightly with heavy string. Trim paper and foil, leaving only about 1 inch overhang. If mold has a lid, place on top.

Place rack in steamer and add boiling water just to bottom of rack. Place mold on the rack. Bring to a boil, then cover with lid. Reduce heat to low and cook at a low boil for 2 hours, adding boiling water occasionally to keep water level just below rack.

Remove mold from steamer. Let rest for about 2 minutes, then remove covers and unmold. Dust generously with confectioners' sugar. Serve plain, with whipped cream or a chocolate sauce. *Yield about 8 servings.*

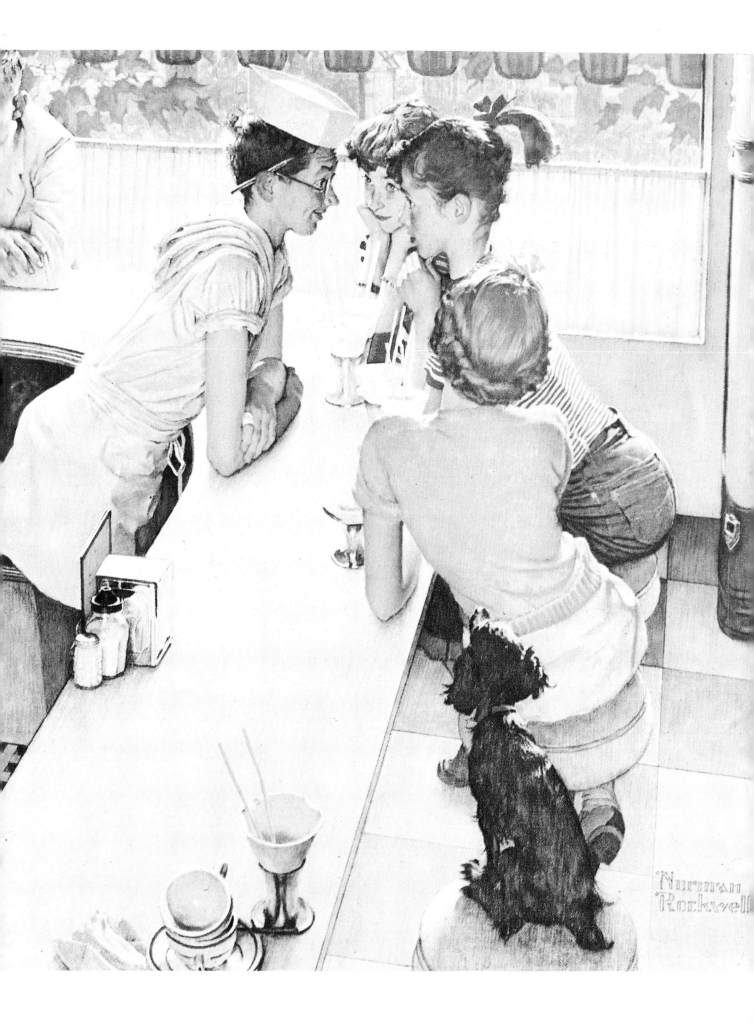

Vermont Maple-Apple Pudding

6   tablespoons butter or margarine
¼   cup brown sugar, firmly packed
1   cup whole-wheat pastry flour
2½ teaspoons baking powder
¼   teaspoon salt
½   teaspoon cinnamon
1   cup milk
½   cup pure maple syrup
½   teaspoon vanilla
3   medium apples (2 cups), peeled and
    coarsely chopped

Melt butter in 2-quart casserole dish.

Stir brown sugar, flour, baking powder, salt, and cinnamon together. Combine milk, syrup, and vanilla. Pour over flour mixture; blend until smooth.

Pour batter over melted butter in casserole; do not stir. Place apples on batter. Bake in 375°F oven 35 to 40 minutes, until crust turns brown. Serve warm with plain cream. *Yield 4 to 6 servings.*

Steamed Molasses Cranberry Pudding

1⅓ cups all-purpose flour
1   cup fresh cranberries, chopped
1   teaspoon baking powder
½   cup molasses
2   teaspoons soda
½   cup hot water

Place ⅓ cup flour in small mixing bowl; then add cranberries. Stir until cranberries are well coated with flour and set aside.

Combine remaining flour with baking powder in separate mixing bowl. Combine molasses, soda, and hot water and stir into flour mixture. Mix until thoroughly blended. Fold in the cranberries.

Spoon into heavily buttered pudding mold. Cover with pudding mold lid or with a double thickness of buttered waxed paper and a double thickness of aluminum foil. Tie securely with string. Place on rack in steamer pan. Add boiling water to halfway of depth of mold. Cover steamer. Steam for 2 hours, adding boiling water as needed to maintain water level.

Remove from steamer. Unmold and serve with Hard Sauce (see Index). *Yield about 6 servings.*

Dolly's Treat - 1924

Holiday Feasts

Easter Dinner

Roast Leg of Lamb

1   (6-pound) leg of lamb
3   teaspoons salt
¼   teaspoon pepper
    Mint jelly *or*

Gravy
2   tablespoons flour
1   bay leaf
1   teaspoon instant minced onion

Wipe lamb with damp cloth; do not remove fell.

Combine salt and pepper; rub all over meat. Insert meat thermometer into fleshy part away from bone. Place on rack in shallow roasting pan. Roast, uncovered, in preheated 325°F oven 2½ to 3 hours, until meat thermometer reads 175°F for medium lamb, 180°F for well-done. Remove to heated platter, keep warm. Serve with mint jelly or gravy.

To make gravy. Pour off drippings; reserve 2 tablespoons in roasting pan. Stir in flour until smooth; gradually stir in 2 cups cold water. Add bay leaf and onion; bring to boiling, stirring constantly. Reduce heat; simmer 5 minutes. Serve hot in gravy boat, along with lamb. *Yield 6 to 8 servings.*

Fresh Asparagus with Cream Sauce

2   pounds fresh asparagus
¼   cup butter
¼   cup all-purpose flour
¾   cup milk
¾   cup half-and-half cream
2   hard-boiled eggs, minced
2   tablespoons fresh lemon juice

Cook asparagus (see Index: Fresh Asparagus); keep warm.

Melt butter in top of double boiler over hot water; blend in flour with wooden spoon. Add milk and cream gradually, stirring constantly. Cook over low heat until smooth and thick. Reserve 1 teaspoon egg; add remainder to sauce; mix well.

Place asparagus in serving dish; sprinkle with lemon juice. Pour sauce in gravy boat; sprinkle with reserved egg. *Yield 4 servings.*

Carrot Mold

12   carrots
½   cup cream
½   cup cracker crumbs
3   tablespoons butter
5   eggs, separated
Salt and pepper to taste

Cook and mash carrots. Add cream, crumbs, butter, beaten egg yolks, salt, and pepper.

Beat egg whites until stiff; fold into mixture. Place in buttered ring mold; set in hot water. Bake in preheated 350°F oven 30 minutes. Turn out mold; fill center with green vegetable for attractive dish. *Yield 6 to 8 servings.*

Cookery is become an art, a noble science; cooks are gentlemen.

Robert Burton 1577–1640

Rice Pilaf

4   tablespoons butter
1   medium onion, finely chopped
1   clove garlic, crushed
1   cup rice
6   coriander seeds
1   stick cinnamon or 1½ teaspoons powdered cinnamon
6   whole cloves or ½ teaspoon ground cloves
    Water or stock

Melt butter in frying pan; cook onion and garlic until soft. Add rice; cook until rice begins to take on color. Add coriander, cinnamon, and cloves. Cover with water, with about ¼ inch water above rice. Simmer gently, covered, until done. If necessary, add a bit of water from time to time to keep rice from sticking. *Yield 5 or 6 servings.*

Polish Easter Cake

½   cup milk
½   cup granulated sugar
½   teaspoon salt
¼   cup butter
¼   cup warm water
1   package active dry yeast
2   eggs, beaten
2½ cups all-purpose white flour
½   cup almonds, chopped
½   cup raisins
½   teaspoon lemon peel, grated
1   cup confectioners' sugar
1   tablespoon milk
    Whole candied cherries

Scald ½ cup milk. Stir in sugar, salt, and butter. Cool to lukewarm.

Pour lukewarm water into large bowl. Sprinkle yeast over water; stir until dissolved. Add milk mixture, eggs, and flour; beat vigorously 5 minutes. Cover; let rise in warm place, free from draft, for 1½ hours or until doubled in bulk.

Stir down batter; beat in almonds, raisins, and lemon peel. Pour batter into greased and floured 1½ quart Charlotte mold or deep cake pan. Let rise 1 hour. Bake in 350°F oven 50 minutes. Let cool in pan 20 minutes; remove.

Beat confectioners' sugar and 1 tablespoon milk together to form glaze.

To serve, place cake on serving platter; drizzle glaze on top. Garnish with cherries. *Yield 8 servings.*

Easter Morning - 1959

Fourth of July Barbecue

Barbecued Chicken with Herb Butter

½ cup dry white wine
2 tablespoons oil
   Juice of ½ lemon
1 small onion, peeled and chopped
½ teaspoon tarragon
1 (3-pound) chicken

Herb Butter
½ cup butter or margarine
4 tablespoons parsley, chopped
2 teaspoons rosemary

Combine wine, oil, lemon, onion, and tarragon. Cut chicken into 8 pieces; put into wine mixture. Leave several hours; turn frequently. Drain.

Put herb butter ingredients into a small pan; heat just enough to melt butter. Use half to baste chicken; put rest into refrigerator to firm.

Brush chicken with half the Herb Butter. Cook on rack over glowing coals, basting several times. Cook until chicken is crisp and golden.

Cut rest of Herb Butter into pats, and serve it on the chicken. *Yield 4 servings.*

Barbecued Corn on the Cob

6   ears corn
    Softened butter
    Salt and pepper to taste

Remove husk and silk from corn; spread generously with softened butter. Sprinkle with salt and pepper; wrap each cob in double thickness of foil, or use heavy-duty foil. Twist ends to seal.

Place on barbecue grid over hot coals. Cook about 20 minutes, turning frequently. *Yield 6 servings.*

Potato Salad

6   large potatoes, peeled and quartered
    Boiling water
½   teaspoon salt
1   medium onion, minced
3   tablespoons vinegar
½   teaspoon prepared mustard
1   teaspoon sugar
2   teaspoons dill seed
    Paprika

In medium saucepan, cook potatoes in boiling salted water until tender. Drain; reserve ¾ cup potato water. Dice potatoes. Add salt and onion; toss gently.

In small saucepan, bring ¾ cup potato water to boil; pour over potatoes and onion. Keep at room temperature 2 to 3 hours. Stir in vinegar, mustard, sugar, and dill seed. (Potato salad will be creamy.) Sprinkle with paprika. Serve at room temperature. *Yield 6 servings.*

What calls back the past, like the rich pumpkin pie?

John Greenleaf Whittier 1807–1892

Vegetable Kebobs with Seasoned Butter Sauce

2   medium zucchini, ends cut off
12   cherry tomatoes
12   fresh mushrooms
½   cup butter, melted
1   tablespoon parsley flakes
¾   teaspoon onion powder
½   teaspoon garlic powder
¼   teaspoon pepper

Cut each zucchini into 6 slices. Arrange tomatoes, zucchini, and mushrooms on 6 skewers.

Pour butter into small bowl. Add parsley flakes, onion powder, garlic powder, and pepper; mix well. Brush over kebobs. Place on grill over hot coals. Cook about 10 minutes, until vegetables are tender. Turn and brush with butter mixture frequently. *Yield 6 servings.*

Marble Brownies

¼   cup butter or margarine
1   cup sugar
2   eggs
⅔   cup cake flour
¼   teaspoon salt
½   cup nuts, chopped
½   teaspoon vanilla extract
2   squares (2 ounces) unsweetened baking chocolate, melted and cooled

Preheat oven to 350°F.

Cream butter. Add sugar; beat until light and fluffy. Add eggs; beat until mixture is smooth. Gradually add flour and salt sifted together. Stir in nuts and vanilla. Pour half the batter into a greased 8-inch baking pan.

Mix chocolate with other half of batter; pour over plain batter. Swirl through with spoon. Bake in preheated 350°F oven 30 minutes. Cool; mark into squares or bars. Cut when cold. *Yield 16 brownies.*

Thanksgiving Dinner

Roast Turkey with Chestnut Dressing

1   (10- to 12-pound) turkey, thawed if frozen

Chestnut Dressing
¼   cup butter or margarine
1   large onion, peeled and chopped
2   stalks celery, chopped
¼   pound ground veal
¼   pound ground pork
1   turkey liver, chopped
¾   teaspoon salt
    Freshly ground black pepper
½   teaspoon Hungarian sweet paprika
6   cups soft bread cubes
¼   cup parsley, chopped
1   pound chestnuts, roasted, skinned, and chopped
1   egg, well beaten

5   slices bacon

Wash turkey well; drain. Remove giblet pack; save liver for dressing. Lightly salt cavity of turkey; set aside while preparing dressing.

Melt butter in large skillet. Add onion and celery; sauté until tender. Using slotted spoon, transfer to large mixing bowl.

Add veal, pork, and liver to skillet; sauté until lightly browned. Season with salt, pepper, and paprika; add to onion mixture. Add remaining stuffing ingredients; mix well.

Stuff turkey with dressing; truss. Place in roasting pan, breast-side-up. Lay bacon strips in single layer over turkey. Roast in preheated 325°F oven approximately 4 hours, to internal temperature of 185°F. Let stand, tented with aluminum foil, 20 minutes before carving.

Make a favorite gravy with pan drippings. *Yield 6 to 8 servings.*

Mashed Potatoes

6   medium potatoes, washed and pared
3   tablespoons butter
1   teaspoon salt
⅓   cup hot milk or cream

Cook potatoes, covered, 20 to 40 minutes in boiling salted water. When tender, drain well; mash with fork or potato masher.

Add rest of ingredients; beat with fork or heavy whisk until creamy. *Yield 6 servings.*

French-Style Green Beans

2   pounds fresh green beans
1   small clove garlic, crushed
¼   cup butter
2   teaspoons salt
⅛   teaspoon pepper, freshly ground
2   teaspoons parsley, finely chopped

Take beans, small bunch at a time, and level them at one end so that tips come together evenly. Cut off both ends so they will be uniform. Use mechanical bean slicer, or cut each bean in half lengthwise with sharp knife. Wash beans; place in top of vegetable steamer. Pour water into base of steamer pan to just below level of top of steamer pan; bring to boil. Add beans; cover. Cook 30 minutes or until beans are crisp-tender.

Remove top steamer pan from base. Pour water from base of steamer pan; turn beans into base. Add garlic, butter, salt, pepper, and parsley; mix well with slotted spoon. Serve immediately.

Beans can be cooked in colander over large saucepan with boiling water, if steamer is not available. *Yield 6 servings.*

Cranberry Holiday Salad

2 cups raw cranberries
1 orange, thinly sliced
1 cup water
¾ cup sugar
1 envelope unflavored gelatin
¼ cup cold water
½ cup seedless grapes, sliced
1 cup celery, diced
¼ cup nuts, chopped

Cook cranberries, orange, and water in covered saucepan until cranberry skins pop open. Press through fine sieve; add sugar and heat to boiling. Soften gelatin in cold water, add hot cranberries, and stir until gelatin is dissolved. Chill until syrupy.

Add remaining ingredients and turn into a ring mold. Chill in refrigerator until firm. Unmold and garnish as desired. *Yield 6 servings.*

Pumpkin Pie

1 unbaked 8-inch pastry shell (see Index: Basic Pastry)
1 cup canned pumpkin
½ teaspoon cinnamon
¼ teaspoon ginger
¼ teaspoon nutmeg
⅛ teaspoon cloves
1 cup milk, half-and-half cream, or evaporated milk
½ cup sugar
1 egg, slightly beaten
½ teaspoon salt

Prepare unbaked pastry shell.

Blend pumpkin and spices thoroughly. Stir in remaining ingredients; mix well. Pour into pastry shell. Bake at 400°F about 1 hour. Pie is done when table knife inserted in center comes out clean. Filling may be soft but will set on cooling. *Yield 6 servings.*

Christmas Dinner

Baked Glazed Ham

1 (12-pound) uncooked cured ham
  Whole cloves
1 cup brown sugar, firmly packed
2 teaspoons dry mustard

Place ham, fat-side up, on rack in roasting pan. Insert meat thermometer in the thickest part of ham without touching the bone. Bake uncovered in preheated 275°F oven for about 6 hours, or until the meat thermometer registers 160°F. (Allow about 30 minutes per pound.)

Remove from oven; with sharp knife, cut off rind, cut diagonal slashes across fat side of ham, in diamond shapes. Place cloves in corners of diamonds. Mix brown sugar, dry mustard, and a little ham fat from roasting pan together; spread over top of ham.

Turn oven up to 400°F; bake ham until brown sugar forms a glaze. *Yield 24 servings.*

Candied Sweet Potatoes

¼ cup butter
6 medium sweet potatoes, cooked and pared
¾ cup grape jam
⅛ teaspoon ground allspice
1 tablespoon orange rind, slivered

Melt butter in large skillet; add potatoes. Top with jam; sprinkle with allspice. Cook, uncovered, over low heat about 20 minutes, basting occasionally. Turn potatoes once. Just before serving, garnish with orange rind. *Yield 6 servings.*

Note: Orange marmalade to which 2 tablespoons honey have been added can be substituted for grape jam.

Minted Peas

1   (10-ounce) package frozen green peas
1   teaspoon dried mint
1   teaspoon sugar
    Boiling salted water
1   tablespoon butter or margarine
    Salt and pepper to taste

Cook peas, mint, and sugar in boiling salted water to cover 5 to 7 minutes, until peas are tender; drain. Stir in butter, salt, and pepper. Serve immediately. *Yield 4 servings.*

Christmas Crullers

3   eggs
⅓   cup sugar
⅔   cup butter or margarine, melted
¼   teaspoon ground cardamom
    Grated rind of 1 lemon
3   tablespoons cream
4   cups flour
    Shortening for deep frying
    Confectioners' sugar for topping

Beat eggs and sugar together until very light. Stir in butter, cardamom, and lemon rind. Add cream and flour. Dough will be quite buttery and easy to handle. Roll dough about ¼ inch thick. Cut with pastry cutter or knife into oblongs 4 inches long, 1 inch wide. Cut slit in middle of each oblong; pull one corner through to make knot. Or just twist oblong to make ribbon effect.

Heat fat to 360°F in skillet. Fry crullers until lightly browned; drain on paper. Store in tightly covered container. Will keep a long time.

When ready to serve, sprinkle with confectioners' sugar. *Yield about 36 crullers.*

Plum Pudding

1   (1-pound) loaf day-old bread
½   pound suet, ground*
1¾   cups all-purpose flour
½   cup brown sugar, firmly packed
1   cooking apple, peeled and chopped
1½   cups golden raisins
1½   cups raisins
1¾   cups currants
2   tablespoon crystallized ginger, minced
2   teaspoons ground allspice
¼   cup almonds, flaked
2   eggs
¾   cup brandy
     Juice of 2 oranges
     Juice of 1 lemon
     Grated rind of 1 orange
     Grated rind of 1 lemon
¼   cup whipping cream

Process bread in blender to make fine crumbs. Place in large mixing bowl. Add prepared suet, flour, brown sugar, apple, raisins, currants, ginger, allspice, and almonds to bread crumbs; mix well. Beat eggs; add brandy, juices, and rinds. Blend into crumb mixture, mixing well; mix in cream. Cover with plastic wrap and refrigerate overnight.

Pack into two 1-quart pudding molds. Cover with buttered waxed paper and foil. Tie securely with string and trim off excess paper and foil. Cover with pudding mold lid. Place in steamer and pour boiling water into steamer, halfway up side of mold. Cover with lid. Steam for 6 hours, adding water to maintain water level, as necessary. *Yield about 15 servings.*

*How to prepare suet: Tear suet into small pieces, discarding only stringy membranes. Chop suet, a small amount at a time, in blender, or grind suet in meat grinder using fine blade.

Index